# YOUR
# HANDSPINNING

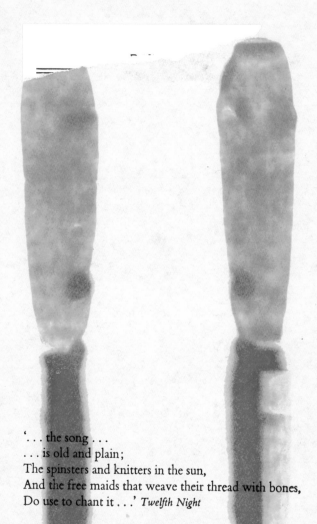

'. . . the song . . .
. . . is old and plain;
The spinsters and knitters in the sun,
And the free maids that weave their thread with bones,
Do use to chant it . . .' *Twelfth Night*

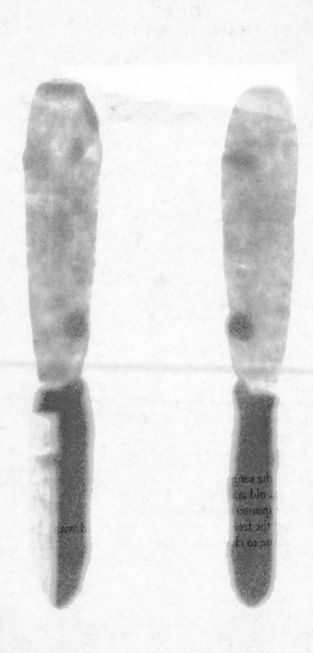

# YOUR HANDSPINNING

*Elsie G. Davenport*

WITH 96 DIAGRAMS
AND
5 PLATES

*Select Books*

5969 WILBUR AVENUE
TARZANA CALIFORNIA 91356

*by the same author*

**YOUR HANDWEAVING**
**YOUR YARN DYEING**

© Copyright 1953 and 1964 by Elsie G. Davenport

FIRST PUBLISHED 1953, Great Britain
REPRINTED 1964, 1968, 1970, 1971, U.S.A.
SBN 910458-01-4

# CONTENTS

# ACKNOWLEDGEMENTS

To Miss E. Sheila MacEwan, for turning pencil sketches into intelligible line drawings and for help and encouragement at all times.

To Miss Ella McLeod, for generous and constructive criticism of the chapters dealing with wool.

To Miss P. Scott, of the National Sheepbreeders' Association, for ready assistance in tracking down elusive information and for providing the specimens of fleece shown in *Plates I* and *V*.

To Mr H. Casparius, for his patience and care in taking and preparing the photographs.

# AUTHOR'S PREFACE

THAT a book on Handspinning should follow one on Weaving is so much a case of putting the cart before the horse that it calls for some explanation.

*Your Handweaving* was written when a great wave of enthusiasm for weaving had almost overwhelmed all the existing organizations able to give reliable information about the craft. All over the country, teachers and others were being asked to give instruction, often at a few weeks notice, in a craft of which they knew next to nothing, and inexperienced instructors and pupils alike had, perforce, to pick up scraps of information – often mis-information – as best they could.

A book of simple technical instruction on the use of the handloom with the materials then available seemed the most urgent need and, judging by the hundreds of appreciative comments and letters received, I still believe the decision made was the right one at the time.

Spinning, dyeing and weaving are but parts of one whole craft and while I would hesitate to say that handweavers should use only yarns they have spun and dyed themselves, there is no doubt at all that the craftsman's joy in his work is most complete when the work has grown in his hands from the beginning.

Until you have seen an experienced spinner at work, you can have no idea of the exquisite refinements of which the craft is capable. I would ask readers to regard this book as an introduction to the craft – an invitation to personal experiment – to be supplemented, whenever possible, by attendance at one of the many demonstrations given nowadays at meetings of Weavers' Guilds, Women's Institutes and County Agricultural Shows.

I hope this book may help readers to that kind of understanding of the craft from which grows love and that some, at least, will experience the extraordinary tranquillity of mind induced by the gentle rhythms of spinning.

1953                                                    ELSIE G. DAVENPORT

PLATE I.

Some typical wools. Shoulder locks from pedigree sheep

| | |
|---|---|
| 1. *Lincoln Longwool.* | 6. *Dartmoor.* |
| 2. *Wensleydale.* | 7. *Southdown.* |
| 3. *Scottish Blackface.* | 8. *Ryeland.* |
| 4. *Exmoor Horn.* | 9. *Suffolk.* |
| 5. *Welsh* (Central Wales) | 10. *Hampshire Down.* |

Length from butt to tip of the Lincoln lock 18 in., and of the South-down lock $1\frac{1}{2}$ in.

### PLATE II.
#### A Kerry Hill fleece laid out for sorting

Chosen for these illustrations because of the strongly marked differences between the several parts of the fleece. Although of Down type, the wool retains some mountain characteristics, notably somewhat coarse tips, seen clearly in *Plate III*. In this fleece, a good deal of the shoulder wool, here laid out in its correct place, just below the figure 1, has been twisted with the neck wool to make the fleece band.

### PLATE III.
Locks removed from points indicated by corresponding numbers in *Plate* II

1. *Shoulder wool* – fine, well-crimped and strong; in this fleece, distributed much as in *Diagram* 2, but extending somewhat further down the back.
2. *Belly wool* (here shorn mostly to right-hand side) – finer than '1', especially at tips, well-crimped but tender.
3. *Back wool* – frothy, somewhat coarser, a little harsher, less strong and resilient than '1'.
4. *Britch wool* – confined to haunches and tail, long, strong, coarse and hairy, containing a little kemp.
5. *Side wool* – longer, straighter and a little less fine than '1', yet very good wool.
6. *Fore-leg wool* – short, coarse and kempy.
7. *Under-neck wool* – very fine, but much rubbed and felted.
8. *Fribbs* (not shown in *Plate* II) – odd clippings and very short butt-end wool resulting from double-cutting when shearing.

PLATE I

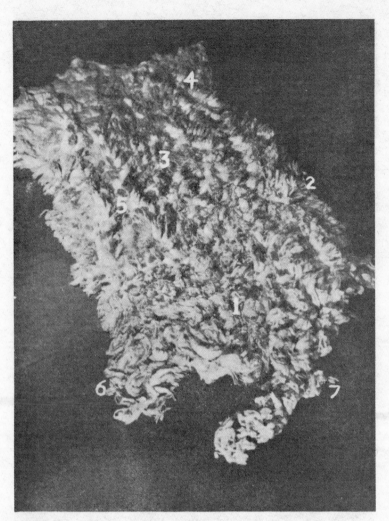

PLATE II

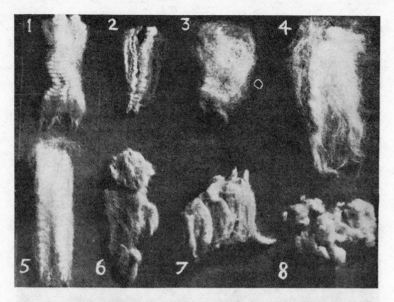

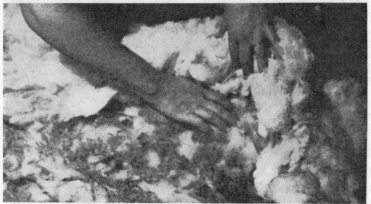

*Above:* PLATE III  *Below:* PLATE IV

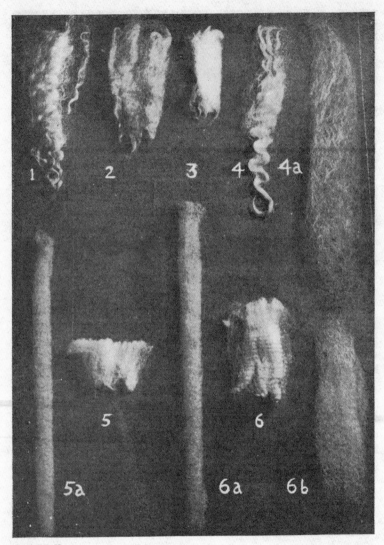

PLATE V

PLATE IV
## Unfolding the fleece

This plate shows clearly the contrast in colour and texture between the light, dense butt-ends and the darker, pointed tips. The fleece has been unrolled and one side unfolded. The right hand holds down the tips of the fleece already laid out while the fold is gently rolled back.

PLATE V.
## Locks and prepared wool

1. *Leicester*, 2. *Border Leicester*, and 3. *Cheviot*, illustrate the effect, on wool, of many years of careful, selective breeding. The long, lustrous, wavy Leicester quality combined with the dense, fine short Cheviot, has given the Border Leicester the best characteristics of both – fineness, lustre, wave and medium length.
4. *Devon Longwool.*
4a. *Devon Longwool* combed for worsted spinning.
5. *Dorset Down.*
5a. *Dorset Down* carded and made into a rolag for woollen spinning.
6. *Romney Marsh* (or *Kent*).
6a. *Romney Marsh* carded and made into a rolag for woollen spinning.
6b. *Romney Marsh* combed for worsted spinning.

Note the longitudinal direction of the wool fibres in the combed wools and the tubular 'spiral spring' arrangement of the fibres in the rolags. The photographs show clearly the even density of the rolags essential for good spinning. Rolag 6a is 11 in. long.

# INTRODUCTION

To many of us, a spinning wheel is a romantic relic of other days, more often associated with antique shops and museums than with any form of practical work; yet, with this simple piece of apparatus we can produce a woollen yarn possessing qualities unobtainable by any other means.

Although this little book on handspinning is written primarily for the use of those intending to become handweavers, spinning is such a delightful occupation that people often find great pleasure in creating yarns for others to weave or knit.

Of all the natural fibres used for spinning, wool is perhaps the least difficult with which to learn. In this country we have a long and honourable tradition for the production and use of wool and it is still the easiest material to obtain in suitable condition for spinning. For this reason wool spinning forms the main subject of this book although there are chapters on the use of linen, silk, various kinds of hair, cotton and synthetic materials. The chapter on British sheep and their fleeces is included in the hope that it will be useful to both town and country readers, helping the former to see that all sheep are *not* alike, encouraging the latter to work with their local wools, at the same time providing them with information about sheep in districts other than their own.

The reader who really desires to learn to spin well is urged to work systematically through the chapters on wool spinning before attempting to use other fibres. Even if one possesses a spinning wheel, one should learn first on a spindle. One cannot correct mistakes in spinning; one must learn to avoid making them. This can be done only by understanding why they have been made and with a spindle it is so much easier to see all that is happening than when trying to control a wheel.

It is perhaps unfortunate that it is so deceptively easy to make a yarn – of sorts – yet so difficult to make a really good yarn unless one is prepared to spend some time making simple practical experiments. Should anyone feel tempted to regard spindle spinning as a form of childish amusement, let him reflect on the gossamer-like fabrics made from spindle-spun yarn which were so vividly depicted by Egyptian tomb painters and sculptors thousands of years ago and, also on the fact that, considerably nearer our own time, the weavers of Ancient Greece used such yarn for the materials whose handle and draping qualities inspired the most wonderful interpretations of textiles in marble the world has yet seen. It must have been a perfect cloth indeed which moved the sculptor of the 'Winged Victory' thus to immortalize the weaver's art — and perfect cloth cannot be made without perfect yarn.

Why, one may ask, should handweavers to-day spin their own yarn? As well ask why a gardener should sow seeds! A cloth which has grown from yarn designed for it gives as much satisfaction to the weaver as a plant grown from seed in a well prepared soil gives the gardener. Both may sometimes purchase their material ready prepared — the weaver his yarn and the gardener his bedding-out plants; each will be a wiser purchaser if he sometimes does the work himself, apart altogether from added pleasure and pride each will feel at having handled something from its beginnings.

To-day, very few handweavers work entirely with handspun yarns. Even if we wish to do so, there are not enough spinners to supply us. For much of our work we must choose from yarns spun by machine for use on power looms which have to work at very high speeds, with as few interruptions as possible, if they are to be profitable. In designing yarns which will stand up to these conditions, valuable characteristics of the fibres from which they are made have to be sacrificed. This is particularly so with wool. Nowadays, too, much blending with synthetic fibres takes place in power spinning, usually in order to cheapen the resulting product. The weaver who lacks practical knowledge of making a yarn cannot hope to avoid the many pitfalls awaiting him in the selection of yarns from among those designed for purposes so different from his own. His hands are insensitive — his eyes are blind; to be able to feel and to see we must spin; only then can we make our choice with confidence. A chapter towards the end of this book is devoted to a discussion of qualities and defects in machine-spun yarns from the hand-weaver's viewpoint.

A chapter is included on the preparation of handspun yarns for weaving and knitting. Fuller details of scouring in preparation for dyeing is given in the volume on Vegetable and Chemical Dyeing in this Series.

## Chapter One

# WOOL

IN the very early stages of man's development he must have discovered that strands of a comparatively weak fibre acquire surprising strength when they are twisted together; but it was not until he found out that by pulling on some of the strands they would slide past one another as they twisted, that he had invented a way of making a strand which was longer as well as stronger than the strands of the original fibre.

Whether he knew it or no, it was one of the greatest occasions in the history of mankind, for he had learned to spin.

The twisting of the fibres while they are being drawn past one another is the basis of all spinning processes. On the manner in which this is done and on the relative positions of the fibres depends all yarn design. The fibres may lie parallel to each other during spinning to give the sleekness of linen yarn or they may lie jumbled and criss-crossed, almost at right-angles to the length of the yarn as in a rough tweed. The fibres may be drawn past one another very regularly – as for a smooth knitting wool, or with planned irregularity – as in a slub yarn. The amount of twist can be very considerable – as in sewing cotton, or very little – as in a linen weft yarn, and, to add to the infinite variety, yarns which have been spun can be spun again to make plied yarns of many kinds.

Whatever the design of the yarn may be, three processes are essential:

(a) Arranging the fibres.
(b) Drawing out the fibres.
(c) Twisting the fibres.

It follows from this simplified explanation of the processes of spinning that smooth fibres are less easy to spin than rough ones because, in the drawing out stage, the smooth fibres will slide past one another all too easily. Linen, silk and cotton fibres are all comparatively smooth, wool fibres are rough.

Seen under a microscope, wool fibres are scaly, looking not unlike the bark of some types of conifers in which the scales overlap in a series of irregular spirals. In addition to being scaly they are also crimped and these two factors greatly assist the spinning because the fibres themselves tend to cling together, a fact which can be demonstrated by twisting a few strands of fleece between the fingers.

The fact that we can so easily make 'a' yarn from wool makes it possible for us to study our actions, when spinning, carefully enough to enable us to acquire the necessary skill and confidence to learn how to make 'the' particular yarn we need – the yarn constructed from a particular fibre in a particular way which we shall use to impart a particular quality to the material made from it.

Without a thorough knowledge of his raw material, a craftsman cannot do good work because he understands only imperfectly the reasons for his actions. Few craftsmen have the privilege of using a more interesting material than wool; few are so intimately concerned with living creatures. Even the wood carver seldom enjoys the pleasure of seeing the living tree wherein he is to find his finished work. It is by no means an unusual experience for a spinner to visualize the yarn, and even the fabric which will grow from it, while his fingers explore the living wool on the back of the sheep.

Nothing is destroyed that his art may flourish; indeed, like all the other whole arts, it takes its place in the natural sequence of living growth; if the wool he uses were not shorn from the sheep, it would be cast by the animal itself in due season.

Though there are many wool-bearing animals whose coats are useful to the spinner, it is with the domestic sheep that we rightly associate the wool most generally used. To those outside the world of farming, the extraordinary variety and diversity of the animals and also of the wool they bear comes as a surprising revelation. Sheep from the British Isles alone give us wool which may be coarse or fine, lustrous or dull, crimped or straight, long or short, soft or harsh according not only to breed, but to character of pasture, vagaries of weather, quality of feeding and a dozen other factors. When we find, in addition to all this, that the wool of every individual sheep contains several varieties, we begin to understand that the selection of the right sort of fleece for a particular piece of work is no light matter and we see why some spinners are content to rely on the experience of the wool supplier or WOOL STAPLER – to give him his correct name – to supply the wool they require.

In spite of the difficulties, the most interesting, and certainly the most instructive way to obtain wool is to make friends with a breeder of pedigree sheep of the breed in which you are interested, and although, at present, he may be beset with regulations, the time will surely soon return when a farmer will be able to dispose of a fleece or two at shearing time without incurring the displeasure of the 'authorities'.

Wool grows on the sheep in definite locks as distinct from the way in which hair grows, for example, on a cat. These locks are the STAPLE, a word which, during our long history, has symbolized the power and dignity of the wool trade. We may be sure that, in whatever setting we may find it, there we shall find some connexion with wool. It occurs in place names, cf. Barnstaple, and it has passed into the currency of every-day speech as a synonym for something essential to well-being, when, for example, we speak of bread as a *staple* article of food.

One lock of wool may be made up of thousands of individual fibres, and to understand the behaviour of wool in the many circumstances in which we shall use it, we must know a little about the construction of these fibres.

The scales of the fibre overlap from the root in the direction of the tip so that the action of stroking the fibre from root to tip smooths them down. This saves the sheep from much annoyance, since burrs, small seeds, bramble thorns and the multitude of other things which are entrapped in the fleece from time to time tend to work out rather than to sink further in.

When the scales are large and flat, the wool is lustrous, and as long stapled wool usually has large scales, length and lustre often go together. In many fine short stapled wools, the scales are small and projecting and this gives a dull surface. The scaly construction of wool gives it the felting quality which is so necessary to the proper finishing of woollen cloths.

The whole length of each fibre is crimped. The best wools have more

than twenty bends per inch and even coarse lustrous wools have a
certain amount. The crimps are not only from side to side along the
length of the fibre, they are also up and down, so that however close may
be the fibres when spun, they can never close up entirely. Herein lies the
virtue of wool for clothing because air is trapped in the spaces between
the fibres in such volume that a woollen yarn has in it more air than
wool! This explains why woollen yarn is so much lighter for its bulk
than any other and also why garments made from it are so warm and
light. It has been calculated that the tightest spun worsted contains only
40 per cent (by volume) of wool, the other 60 per cent is air! The crimp,
which nothing can entirely destroy, is responsible for the extreme
resilience of woollen yarn. This resilience the handspinner alone can
preserve unimpaired and it allows a well spun, well woven cloth to
retain its shape under almost any conditions of wear.

Most sheep grow hair as well as wool; the hair is known to wool
staplers as KEMP. Some of the best wool-bearing breeds are almost
entirely free from kemp, but some may be expected in most British
breeds, especially those from the hill lands. In our enthusiasm for wool
as a material, we sometimes forget that to the sheep who bears it, it is a
thatch grown to protect it from the particular climate it must endure.
Rain runs more easily off hair than off wool, so kemp increases in wet
districts.

At the base of each fibre of wool is a small oil gland which lubricates
it during growth. This oiliness greatly facilitates spinning and is the
reason why the handspinner seldom washes the fleece unless he wishes
to dye it for making mixture yarns. Freshly shorn fleece is delightful to
spin because the oil is still soft; later, olive oil must be sprinkled on to re-
soften it. Close to the root of the fibre is the sweat gland which deposits
SUINT on the surface of the fibre. This is also greasy, but when fleece has
been stored for some time, it becomes hard and almost powdery. All
this natural oil accounts for a considerable proportion of the weight of
the fleece, sometimes nearly a third, and if the sheep has not been washed
before shearing it may well be greater than this.

Nowadays, the quality of wool is indicated by a system of numbering,
from 100 downwards, which is related to the degree of fineness to which

it is possible to spin it by the WORSTED method (see *Chapter Five*). Briefly, this means that from 100s quality wool, 100 hanks each consisting of 560 yards of yarn, could be spun to weigh 1 lb. This is extremely fine and is only possible with the very best Merino fleece. Wool from the British Isles ranges from 56–60s in the best Down breeds to 28s in some Mountain sheep. The system of numbering is directly connected with the requirements of the power spinners and while it serves as a general guide to the fineness of the wool, the handspinner should not imagine that only the high numbered grades are worthy of his attention. As a matter of fact, Merino wool of very high quality is extremely difficult for any but experienced spinners to use, while Welsh wool, graded nowadays as 40–50s, is not only easy to spin but makes a variety of excellent yarns.

And now, in the hope that many of my readers will one day experience for themselves the satisfaction of wearing, as I do as I write, a comfortable garment, woven from wool they have spun and dyed, from the fleece of a sheep they have helped to rear out of a flock they have known and loved, may I introduce the animal on which the fertility and prosperity of Britain was built.

*Chapter Two*

## SHEEP

OF all the sheep in the world, the MERINO produces the finest wool. Originally a smallish animal with poor meat qualities, it is thought to have been introduced into Spain from North Africa by the Moors, and, in the Middle Ages, the Spaniards valued the breed so highly that attempts to send any out of the country were punishable by death. During the eighteenth century, however, numbers were sent as royal gifts to various parts of Europe and because the flocks from which they came were migratory sheep (in Spanish, *ovejas marinas*) wandering, like many of our own mountain breeds, from one feeding ground to another, they came to be known as Merinos.

One flock was given to the Elector of Saxony and founded a tradition for fine wool which persists to-day in the use of the name 'saxony' to describe a mixed wool of very fine quality. Another flock went to the farm of Louis XVI at Rambouillet, where their much improved descendants flourish still; their blood and their name persists in some of the great flocks of the U.S.A. At about the same time as the flock was founded in Saxony, a number were sent to George III who kept them for some time at Kew. These were used to improve many of our own breeds before being sent to South Africa, where the climate was more suited to them.

From one source or another, there is Merino blood in the flocks of all the great wool producing areas in the world, mostly crossed with good meat breeds from this country. Though they have been used here in the past to improve our wool, our climate does not suit them and they have been bred here only experimentally. Merino wool is very fine, very crimpy, with an average quality of 70–90s.

Until the eighteenth century, sheep were bred in this country mainly for their wool. Next in importance was their milk, for making cheese, and their skins, for leather and parchment; only incidentally were they regarded as meat producers. In certain parts of the country, their meat was quite unacceptable as food and this, perhaps, gave rise to the distinction still made by many people in the North of England between 'meat' and 'mutton'. With the rise in the standards of living in towns, which accompanied the Industrial Revolution, came an increased demand for meat, and during the eighteenth and nineteenth centuries sheep were improved in size, at first without much detriment to wool.

Increasing use of cotton and silk and growing world wool production eventually caused a steadily decreasing demand for British wool, and for many years now more and more attention has been devoted to the development of mutton character at the expense of wool quality. At the present time, the effects of this policy – which conditions since 1939 have done nothing to mitigate – are all too apparent in the lack of stability of breed types of fleeces. However, there are, at the time of writing, signs that world demand and better prices may make it worth while for the British sheep farmers to give more consideration to their wool crop than they have done for many years.

The early ancestors of our domestic sheep were almost certainly small goat-like creatures, probably brown in colour, closely related to the Moufflon which is native to some Mediterranean areas and of which there are examples in the London Zoological Gardens. Some of our hill breeds bear unmistakable traces of this ancestry in the fine horns, delicate powerful feet and – among the Welsh hills – an incidence of sheep with pale golden faces and legs, colloquially known to the border sheepmen as 'tea drinkers'. On the island of Soay, in the Hebrides, too, there is a small flock of little brownish sheep which have been bred unmixed with alien blood from time immemorial. In the course of centuries, many different types have been introduced with each successive wave of invaders who came and settled and there are now more than forty different British breeds.

## TERMS USED TO DESCRIBE SHEEP

The words used to describe sheep of different age and sex vary in detail up and down the country. Lambs are EWE lambs if female; if male, they are TUP or RAM lambs (Tup in the North, Ram in the South).

If castrated – i.e. for fattening as meat as distinct from rearing to breed from – they are WETHER or WEDDER lambs.

After weaning, at five months old, they become ewe, tup or wether HOGGS, HOGGETTS or TEGS. Note that hogg (double 'g') is a sheep, not a pig.

At about fifteen months old, in the spring or early summer – depending on district climate – they are shorn for the first time. The females then become THEAVES, THAVES or THREAVES in the South, GIMMERS in the North. The males are then called SHEARLING or DIAMOND tups or rams or, in some districts, DINMONTS.

In the autumn, the females are mated with the ram and have their lambs in five month's time. When, a few months later, they are shorn again, they become TWO-SHEAR (or TWO TOOTHED) ewes. Thereafter each shearing denoting an additional year of her age, she becomes three-, four-, shear ewe. After the age of four, age can no longer be proven because she grows no more teeth; when they wear out and she can no longer graze, she is sold as BROKEN MOUTHED and turned into meat.

Hogg wool is the best, and though wether hoggs give the biggest yield, the fleece of the ewe hogg is of better quality. The wool of sheep slaughtered for meat reaches the market as FELL wool; in spite of many assertions to the contrary, modern methods of removing it from the skins by means of chemical action are detrimental to the quality.

The usual classification of our sheep into MOUNTAIN, LONGWOOLS and DOWNS, is that which emphasizes the character of their native surroundings and, in consequence, the character of the covering they grow to protect them.

In all the following notes, the quality number follows the name of the breed. It is generally accepted that this number refers to the best part of the fleece. (See *Chapter Three*.)

MOUNTAIN BREEDS. These are sheep of the hills around and over the 1,000 ft. line. They are small, giving excellent meat, very hardy and the fleeces are strong, coarse, medium to long in staple and often kempy. The extreme humidity of our mountainous districts produces wools peculiar to this country and attempts to maintain its character in flocks exported to various parts of the world have been unsuccessful.

†*Scottish Blackface*. 28–40s. Native to the 'black' hills (heather covered) of Scotland. Once a breed of open heaths, they can find a living where even Welsh Mountain sheep would die. According to some authorities, they came westward from Central Asia with the very early migrations of man. The coarse, almost strawlike fleeces, 8–12 in. in staple, are excellent for carpet wool. Flocks bred in the Highlands and Hebrides have softer fleeces, the best being used for Harris and similar tweeds. Fleece weight, 3–4 lb.

†*Cheviot*. 48–54s. Native to the Cheviot hills, they are generally found on the 'green' (not heather-covered hills) of Scotland. Descended, like the Welsh, from the old tan-faced sheep, they were improved in the eighteenth century with Merino and Southdown rams and later with Leicester and Lincoln blood. Their present excellence largely results from years of careful selection within the breed. They are white-faced, Roman nosed, with close, white, compact wool of crisp handle and a staple length of 4 in., which is delightful for handspinning.

On the green hills of the Highlands and in Sutherland and Caithness, the breed has developed a distinctly different type as a result of the introduction of Spanish Merino blood early in the nineteenth century. The fleece is softer, finer and not so sharp in handle. Cheviot fleeces weigh 4–4½ lb.

*Cotswold*. 44s. This very old breed has become very rare; though they may still be found on the bleak hills of the Gloucester Cotswolds, only one pure-bred flock exists to-day. The wool, though lustrous, is rather coarse and crisp. Fleeces weigh 7–8 lb.

*Dalesbred*. 32/40s. This sheep is a native of the dales in the central area of the Pennines and has been bred on the original hill sheep of the district. The fleece is fairly long in staple, free from black and with a coarse outer coat covering finer dense wool beneath; it weighs 4–6 lb.

*Derbyshire Gritstone*. 46s. A very old breed, native to the Derbyshire Peak district, which may have originated in * Lonk x Down. The sheep

† Indicates that fleece is shown in *Plates I – V*.

* x=crossed with: a hardy breed is usually 'improved' by mating the ewes with a ram of the breed having the desired qualities.

have speckled faces, ears and legs; the fleece, 6–8 in. in staple, is fairly
fine and dense, but with some long grey and black hair and weighs
4–4½ lb.

†*Exmoor Horn.* 48/50s. These sheep live on the moors and hills of West
Somerset and North Devon and derive from an old forest breed improved by crossing with Down rams. The wool is 3–4 in. in staple,
lustrous, soft, with good felting qualities and excellent for handspinning.
Fleeces weigh 4 lb.

*Herdwick.* 32/40s. The predominant breed in the Lake District. Very
hardy and resourceful, they are said to have been introduced by the
Norsemen. They are mentioned in the twelfth-century records of
Furness Abbey, but the legend that their ancestors swam ashore from a
wrecked Spanish galleon has no foundation. The fleece, 6–8 in. in staple,
is harsh and full of kemp, variable in colour and weighs 3–4 lb.

*Lonk.* 44s. Rather larger than most Mountain sheep, native to the
Pennines (North Derbyshire, East Lancashire, West Yorkshire), it can
stand very severe weather, even surviving long burial in drifts. Fleeces
are 8 in. or so in staple, soft and full in handle, white and with little
kemp. Average weight: 5–8 lb.

*Pennistone.* 36s. Another sheep of the Pennines (South Yorkshire and
Cheshire border), it is a strange-looking animal with a rough fleece and
a large, muscular tail. The long stapled, harsh fleece weighs from
4–4½ lb.

*Radnor.* 40–50s. Native to the hills of Radnor Forest, originally
developed from the Welsh by crossing with Shropshires, it is a smallish,
hardy sheep. The wool is finer than Welsh, but is kempy and there is
always some grey hair. Fleeces weigh 4–5 lb.

*Rough Fell.* 40–32s. This is a horned sheep native to the high fells of
Westmorland and has been bred there for centuries. It is also found
in the West Riding of Yorkshire. The wool is 9–10 in. in staple, harsh,
white, very strong and with the softer 'undercoat' so common in longwooled mountain sheep. Fleeces weigh 5–6 lb.

*Swaledale.* 40–42s. This breed may have originated from Blackfaced x
Wensleydale rams or may have developed as a natural, local variant of
the black-faced hill sheep native to the northern Border country. Fleeces

are regular, 4–7 in. in staple, hard in handle and weigh about 5 lb.

†*Welsh Mountain*. 32–50s. They are small, very active sheep that no fences yet invented can keep in – or out! They live on the Welsh hills above the 1,000 ft. line. Rams are horned, ewes hornless; they give excellent meat. Fleeces in some areas are very kempy; there is considerable variation in colour, often including much grey. Most flocks produce some all-black sheep and a black strain is now established as a separate breed. Wool is soft, with good felting qualities and a staple length of 3–4 in. It is an excellent wool for handspinners and fleeces weigh 2–3½ lb.

*Shetland*. These are not strictly mountain sheep. They are native to Orkney and Shetland and are small goat-like creatures; the lambs are so tiny that they can, and do, shelter from the cold, wet wind in a rabbit hole. The climate is perpetually moist and the sheep grow an outer coat of hair in addition to the exquisitely fine, soft wool. The sheep are not shorn; the wool is 'rooed', i.e. plucked, in July. It is sad that the decline in demand for this very beautiful wool, coupled with the drive to produce more meat, has led to the introduction of Blackfaces and Cheviots and the pure-bred Shetland is fast disappearing. No wool is more rewarding for the handspinner and knitter.

LONGWOOLS. These are the breeds of the richer, grassy lowlands and the coastal plains. Their wool is long, lustrous and somewhat coarse. In earlier times, the longwooled sheep of the Midlands gave the fleece which was combed and spun by the WORSTED process (*Chapter Five, page* 54) for use on the family looms.

†*Lincoln*. 44–36s. This is one of the largest sheep in the world. It is found in Lincolnshire and on the East Yorkshire coast. The wool is dense, lustrous, rather wavy and very long in staple – up to 26 in. There are some flocks in Nottinghamshire which have bred finer fleeces, sometimes known as 'Nottingham wool'. Fleeces average 16–17 lb. and have been known as heavy as 28 lb. The Corriedale breed of New Zealand was developed from Lincoln x Merino with some Leicester blood.

†*Leicester*. 44s. It has been suggested that the Flemish weavers, who were brought to England by Edward III, introduced sheep with long, lustrous wool and that on descendants of these, Bakewell, the great Leicestershire

breeder of the eighteenth century, founded the Leicester. They are now found chiefly in the East Riding of Yorkshire, where they are much used for crossing with hill breeds. The fleece has a staple of 11–12 in.; it is fine, lustrous, wavy, and extremely uniform; average weight is 10–14 lb.

†*Border Leicester*. 48–44s. The eighteenth-century Leicesters were crossed with Cheviots on the Scottish border to produce an almost new breed. Long bodied, and with the aristocratic face of the Leicester, they are much used for crossing on Cheviot ewes to produce the *Half-bred*, the wool of which is used in the Galashiels wool trade. Border Leicester rams are used on Blackfaces to give the *Greyface*. Border Leicester gives coarse, fat meat, but is used on Merino types overseas to produce excellent mutton. The fleeces are lustrous, shorter in staple and closer than the Leicester and weigh 9–12 lb.

†*Dartmoor*. 32–36s. These sheep are natives of the moors of Devon and Cornwall and have been improved, at some time, with Leicester blood. The wool is 10–12 in. in staple, coarse, somewhat lustrous and curly, generally not kempy. Fleeces weigh 10–16 lb.

Whitefaced Dartmoors give shorter finer fleeces of about the same weight.

†*Devon Longwool*. 32s. These have been bred from the native *Nott*, improved with Leicester blood. They are found on the higher pastures all over Devon. The wool is dense, wavy, fairly lustrous, 12 in. in staple and very strong. Fleeces weigh 14 lb.

*South Devon*. 32–36s. Fleeces rather similar to above but finer, denser and more lustrous; they weigh 18–20 lb.

†*Kent or Romney Marsh*. 50–46s. A breed of Flemish origins and with Leicester blood, which, in the course of many years, has developed characteristics which fit it perfectly for its native environment. It stands up to the cold driving rain, its hooves have become adapted to the marshy ground and, for these reasons, the breed is widely imported into South Island, New Zealand and also into the Falkland Islands. The wool is closer, finer but less lustrous and with more definite crimp than most longwools. It has good felting qualities and is very useful to the handspinner. Fleeces weigh 7–8 lb.

†*Wensleydale*. 44s. These are sheep of the high dales running through

the West Yorkshire moors. They originated from the old native Tees-water breed crossed with Leicesters. The wool is very lustrous, curly, and grows in ringlets with a staple length of 10–12 in. Fleeces weigh 11 lb.

Wensleydale rams are used on Swaledale ewes to produce the *Masham*, which takes its name from the North Yorkshire town. The wool is of medium length, kind in handle, and is known in Scotland as 'Yorkshire Cross'; the fleeces weigh about 8 lb. Mashams are also found in parts of Cumberland and Westmorland.

DOWN BREEDS. These sheep are native to the lower hills, downs, and sometimes forests, in the true meaning of the word, i.e. open woodland and wide, treeless heath. They give excellent, lean mutton and fine short wool, although the wool is less fine and short in those breeds which have spread to hill country approaching the 1,000 ft. line, where rainfall is higher.

†*Southdown*. 60–56s. This breed is native to the chalk hills around Lewes. Originally very small, it was much improved by the great Ellman of Glynde by a process of careful selection. It is the finest English wool, very short in staple, very close and very crimped. It is rather short for worsted spinning machinery but is excellent material for the experienced handspinner for both woollen and worsted methods. Fleeces weigh 3½–4½ lb.

†*Suffolk*. 56s. These were produced from an old Norfolk breed crossed with Southdown. They are now black-faced and black-legged, with a dense fleece which whitens as the animals mature, though there are always some dark hairs. The wool is crisp, soft, crimped, white, not so fine as Southdown with a staple length of 3½ in. Fleeces weigh about 6 lb.

†*Hampshire Down*. 56s. This is one of the larger Down breeds. Originally obtained by crossing an old local breed with Southdown and Wiltshire Horn. The fleeces are neither so fine nor so uniform in colour as Southdown. Length of staple is 3½ in. and the fleece weight is 6–8 lb.

†*Dorset Down*. 54s. These sheep were bred from a native Down sheep x Hampshire Down and probably improved with Southdown blood. The wool is 3–4 in. in staple, close and fine. Fleeces weigh about 5–6 lb.

*Wiltshire Horn*. This is a sheep bearing practically no wool. Flocks are to be seen now mainly in Anglesey, Buckinghamshire and Northamptonshire and they are used almost entirely for improving size in Mountain breeds for meat.

*Dorset Horn.* 50s. This is an old breed developed from the earlier Wiltshire Horn. Records of 1793 suggest an even earlier crossing with the older Southdown. In 1817, careful selective breeding began and it is now popular in its native county and also in Somerset and the Isle of Wight. Ewes will lamb twice a year – a practice not encouraged by good breeders. The wool is fine, white, 3–4 in. in staple, crisper than Southdown and has good felting qualities. Fleeces weigh $4\frac{1}{2}$–6 lb.

*Devon Closewool.* 46–50s. This is a breed native to the hills and pastures of Exmoor and the surrounding country on the Devonshire side. The wool is close and fairly fine, 3–4 in. in staple length. It is most useful to the handspinner for making tweed yarn. Fleeces weigh 7–8 lb.

†*Ryeland.* 54s. This is not, strictly speaking, a Down sheep; it is a native of the former hungry, rye growing lands of Herefordshire and is one of the very old breeds. In the Middle Ages, Ryeland fleeces were known as 'Lemster ore'; such was the prosperity they brought to the wool market of the ancient town of Leominster. At some time in the eighteenth century, Merino blood was introduced and the wool is now soft, close, free from black hair, strong, with a staple length of $3\frac{1}{2}$ in. The addition of Leicester and Shropshire blood in later years has improved the meat but with some detriment to the wool. Fleeces weigh 8–10 lb.

*Shropshire.* 50–54s. A breed of somewhat mixed origins developed from the old native *Morfe*, now extinct, and from a black-faced sheep once found on Cannock Chase. It now has Southdown, Leicester and, some say, Cotswold blood. The wool is medium stapled, about 4 in., regular, crisp, with some grey hairs. Fleeces weigh 7–8 lb.

*Oxford Down.* 48–50s. This, the largest Down sheep, was developed as recently as last century from Cotswold x Hampshire with some Southdown blood. Both meat and wool are the coarsest of the Down breeds and Longwool influence is obvious. Fleeces have a staple length of 4–5 in., are curly, soft in handle, with much grey hair and are often much liked by handspinners; they weigh 8–10 lb.

†*Kerry Hill.* 50s. In appearance, one of our most beautiful sheep. It is

native to the hills of the Central Wales border and may derive from
Welsh Mountain with Ryeland blood. The face is long, white and
smooth, with eyebrows delicately marked with black and a black nose
and mouth. Fleeces are very white, crisp, fairly fine, free from grey and
with a staple length of 4 in. Sheep from exposed pastures sometimes grow
a fair amount of kemp. Weight 4–7 lb.

*Clun Forest.* 50s. This is a black-faced, black-legged sheep, native to
the hills around Clun on the Shropshire–Wales border. Owing to their
good early maturing mutton qualities, they are also fairly common in
the West Midlands. Fleeces are very similar to Kerry, though neither so
white nor so long; they weigh 4–6 lb.

The above list is by no means exhaustive; there are many interesting,
though purely local breeds about which little is known outside their
native area. There are, for example, Manx sheep about which the writer
has sought in vain for information.

Breeds also exist within breeds, so to speak. Welsh flocks on the
southern hills of the Principality yield very different wool from those
in the Snowdon district, and wool from the Plynlimmon area is different
again.

A curiously interesting breed which can be found as far apart as
Dorset and Herefordshire is the Jacob's Sheep. It is said to have originated
in the flock which Jacob bred with such ingenuity out of Laban's flock.
The story is vividly told in Genesis xxix and the sheep are undoubtedly
Eastern in appearance, with one pair of straight horns projecting forwards
and a second pair curled round the sides of the head. The fleeces are of
Mountain type – coarse, fairly long, and boldly speckled black-and-
white.

No one person can hope to be really familiar with all breeds of sheep
in this country, and suggestions for additions – or correction of errors –
for inclusion in later reprintings will be heartily welcome.

*Chapter Three*

## SORTING A FLEECE

HAVING obtained a fleece – what next? If it is a good example of the breed, we might expect that all the wool would be more or less as described in the preceding chapter. In fact, nothing is less likely; the British fleece which is uniform all through is a rarity in any breed.

Country readers will, I am sure, forgive me for pointing out some facts about sheep well known to them, that town-dwellers may have little chance of observing. Sheep spend their lives out of doors in all weathers. Rain, wind, hot sun alike beat down on their backs; they may be buried in snow in a hard winter and starved of grass in a hot, dry summer. Except when sheltering lambs, they invariably turn their backs to 'the weather'. Hill and mountain sheep often travel through long rough grasses, heather and burrs, bracken and sometimes brambles. Sheep which have fed from troughs rub neck and chest wool against the edges and grains of chaff and other matter become imbedded in the fleece. Pitch or marking paint is used, often in what appears to the spinner to be excessive quantities, frequently alas, on the best parts of the fleece. In any breed, sudden checks in growth caused by illness or by a period of poor feeding can be read in weak places in the length of the staple – near the tip if the check came soon after the previous shearing, near the root if within a month or so of the wool being shorn.

All these factors affect either the condition or the character of growth of the wool – sometimes both – in the various parts of the fleece. The greater the variation in climate, the more marked the differences are likely to be, so that, given equally high standards of feeding and breed, wool on a Southdown from Sussex will, in all probability, be more uniform in character than wool on a Shropshire Down from the more variable climate of the Welsh border, with its greater extremes of temperature and rainfall.

From the above, the reader will understand that the best wool is likely to be found where it has least weathering, least wear from rubbing and where wet runs off quickly – namely on the shoulders; that the harshest wool will be found at the back and that, in the lower parts especially, it may be strong and·coarse especially in hill breeds.

Wool sorting terms vary not only according to whether for woollen or worsted spinning, but also in different parts of the country. The three systems of nomenclature known to the author are set out in the following table which should be studied in conjunction with *Diagrams 1* and *2*.

Wool sorting is a highly skilled craft which takes the best part of a life-

## WOOL SORTING TERMS

| Part of Animal | Kind of Wool | Worsted Trade | Woollen Trade | Traditional |
|---|---|---|---|---|
| Shoulder. | Best quality. | Fine. | Picklock. | Super diamond. |
| Sides. | Not quite so fine or regular. | Neat. | Prime. | Extra diamond. |
| Neck. | Fine, shorter, perhaps irregular. | Blue. | Downrights. | Shafty. |
| Back. | Less close and strong than shoulder. | Choice. | Choice. | Diamond. |
| Haunches. | Coarse, long, usually strong. | Abb. | Abb. | Prime. Britch. |
| Round tail. | Very coarse, dirty, often kempy. | Britch. | Britch. | Tail or britch. |
| Belly. | Fine, short, tender, sometimes felted. | Seconds. | Seconds. | Picklock. |
| Forelegs. | Short, irregular, poor. | Brokes. | Brokes. | Brokes. |
| Hind legs. | Coarse, hairy, strong. | Cowtail. | Brown. | Britch. |
| Head. | Sometimes very coarse and hard, sometimes as good as back wool. | Top knot. | Poll lock. | Poll lock. |

time to learn; all that can be attempted here is to guide the reader along general lines which will help him to learn from his own practical experience. At the same time, he is urged to take any opportunity he may find to see a practical demonstration.

A good breeder takes a pride in having his fleeces well folded after shearing. They are tied up with a band made by pulling out the neck wool, putting a twist into it and winding it round the folded fleece with the end neatly tucked in (*Diagrams 3, 4* and *5*). Fleeces are always folded in three lengthwise, with the shorn ends outwards, as in *Diagram 3*. Some shearers cut the belly wool all to one side, some shear down the middle, leaving half on each side; the same applies to the under-neck wool.

If you are preparing to sort a fleece at home, spread as large an area of floor space as possible with newspaper or, if possible, when the weather is dry and not windy, work out of doors: good light is essential. A fleece, once off the sheep's back, occupies an incredible amount of space and a big Longwool fleece has to be split down the centre of the back for sorting. Have beside you boxes or newspaper and string for keeping the sortings or MATCHINGS separate, also a pencil and gummed paper for labelling.

I. OPENING OUT. Find the end of the neck band and undo it carefully; then untwist the band. Unroll the bundle slowly, parting the fibres gently and, when the full length is unrolled, unfold it. If your fleece comes direct from a breeder, this process should not be difficult, but fleeces obtained from wool staplers nowadays are often very badly packed, tied round with string, instead of with the neck band, and having had pieces torn out from various parts. (If, at this stage, you feel doubtful about your fleece, read to the end of the chapter before handling it further.)

When the fleece is fully opened, it should look more or less like *Diagram 2*. At this stage, study *Plates II, III* and *IV*. Tucked into the middle of the fleece you will probably find odds and ends of short, possibly dirty wool, trimmings from legs, tail, etc. They are useful for colour matching when dyeing. When the fleece is properly laid out, all the tips of the wool will be upwards.

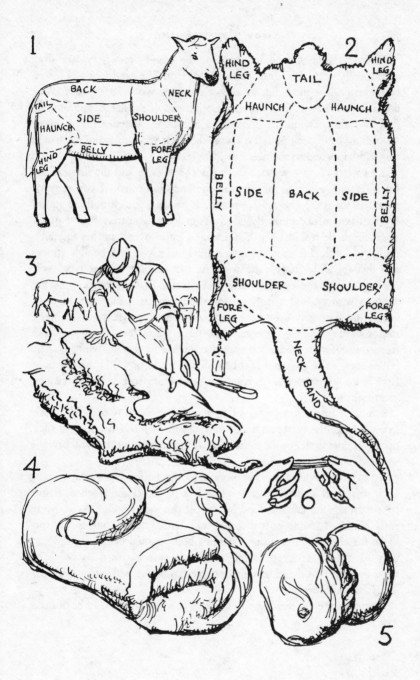

1

BACK
NECK
SIDE
SHOULDER
TAIL
HAUNCH
HIND LEG
BELLY
FORE LEG

2

HIND LEG
TAIL
HIND LEG
HAUNCH
HAUNCH
BELLY
SIDE
BACK
SIDE
BELLY
SHOULDER
SHOULDER
FORE LEG
FORE LEG
NECK BAND

3

4

6

5

Untwist the neck band and examine the whole fleece very carefully; occasionally shearers use the coarse wool from the hind legs and lower back (britch) for the band, instead of the neck wool. If the band wool is coarser and harder than that at the other end of the fleece, you may be fairly certain that this has been done. Sometimes, part of the shoulder wool may have been pulled up with the neck wool to make the band; this had happened to the fleece in *Plate II*.

2. EXAMINING THE WOOL. With the above table and the illustrations for reference, examine the wool in the areas indicated; if you remove a lock to see it closely, replace it and, at present, detach nothing more. If you have an exceptionally good hogg fleece, you may find it much the same all over, with only the skirtings – legs, lower haunches and tail – noticeably different. It is more than likely that you will be able to see, and feel the differences quite well. As the amount of best wool will depend on the breeding, feeding and general living conditions of the sheep, you may find it only on the shoulders, or it may extend right across and part way down the back; a poorer type of the same breed might have good wool only on the upper shoulders. Compare locks from the different areas with special reference to the following points: (1) Fineness, (2) Crimpiness, (3) Length, (4) Strength, (5) Lustre (particularly in Longwools), and (6) Kindliness of handle (soft or harsh, wiry or yielding).

N.B. The professional way of testing for strength is to hold a lock extended tightly between finger and thumb of each hand, then flick up the middle finger of the right hand. If the staple is weak it will break – very difficult! (*Diagram 6.*)

3. SORTING. Work from the poorer to the better wool and as each lot is sorted off it should be put into a box or parcel and labelled. Begin by removing the tail and hind leg wool; this will be suitable for your early efforts at spinning. It is strong and hard-wearing, but usually too harsh for clothing. If the sheep has not been washed before shearing, it may have dung attached. While this in no way harms the wool (it is quite the best scouring agent!), the fleece can be washed before spinning (see *Chapter Eleven*).

Next remove the fore leg wool, which in some breeds may be of little use except for dyeing samples, and then take the wool from the haunches. You may find similar wool extending right across the back from haunch to haunch, but in the centre of the back it may be weaker.

Now take off the belly wool which will be soft and fine. It may be felted and a little dirty; it is not strong, but should make good soft weft yarn.

Remove the under-neck wool and, as you are approaching the best wool, take some care in deciding where this begins; in some breeds it may include the upper-neck wool. The determination of these vague boundaries is very difficult for the inexperienced sorter, and careful study should be made of the photographs and accompanying notes.

You are now left with the wool from the sides, the shoulders and the forward part of the back. Probably the side wool will be less fine and dense than the shoulder wool, and the wool on the back will almost certainly be weaker than either, though it may be no shorter. If you can distinguish no differences in what is left, carefully remove any traces of paint or tar, shake out straw or any other foreign matter and set this good wool aside for future use. If you are able to sort it further into two or three grades, it is wise to do so.

Some breeds have greyish wool mixed with the white; if you may be dyeing bright, clear colours, this must be removed. This should be watched for in all Mountain breeds and occurs quite often in the following Down breeds: Hampshire, Suffolk, Shropshire, Oxford and Dorset Down.

All Mountain sheep and some Down sheep bred in wet areas have a certain amount of kemp and as this, apart from its harshness, has a poor affinity for some dyestuffs, it must be removed during sorting from wool intended for wearing apparel. It is not generally found in the areas of finest wool.

Some fleeces, notably the Welsh, yield a variety of colours; these can be sorted for use as distinct colour schemes, or set aside for blending. These natural colours are usually fairly, though not entirely, fast to light.

4. RESULTS OF POOR SORTING. Careful sorting is essential to successful work whether in spinning, dyeing, knitting or weaving. The following are some difficulties arising from bad sorting:

(a) *Unevenness in spinning* because different parts of the fleece handle so differently.

(b) *Dyeing not level* because different parts of the fleece have different affinity to dyestuffs.

(c) *Bad tension in knitting* when wool with varying amount of crimp has been used in the same yarn; garments distorting in shape after washing because wool with different shrinkage rate has been used in the same garment.

(d) *Difficult warps for the weaver.* Breaks will result from the use of weaker parts of the fleece for warp yarns; tension will be uneven if wools with differing amounts of crimp are used in parts of the warp. For the same reason, bad weft tension will spoil the selvedges since the amount of crimp controls the extent to which a yarn will stretch and relax; where the crimp is greatest, the weft yarn will 'draw in'.

(e) Most heartbreaking of all, bad sorting may show for the first time when the material is being finished because the felting qualities on which all finishing processes depend may vary very much in different parts of a fleece.

5. SORTING A BADLY PACKED FLEECE OR PART OF A FLEECE. Having read the preceding paragraphs, lay the wool out as carefully as possible and take out any which is markedly coarser and harsher than the rest. Next remove any which is obviously finer and more crimped than what is left. Sort the rest into two or three piles of like wool; then examine each pile with reference to *par. 2* above.

6. STORING FLEECE. However dirty or greasy a fleece may be, it is easier to keep in good condition unwashed. It should be stored in a cool dark place which must be dry. In a closely fastened box, or wrapped in several sheets of newspaper, it can be kept free from moth if sprinkled with crystals of paradichlorbenzine.

*Chapter Four*

## LEARNING TO MAKE A CONTINOUS YARN

BEFORE one can begin to learn to spin, one must learn how to gain sufficient confidence to make a continuous yarn. This one can do most easily with a very primitive piece of equipment, the spindle. It can be made fairly easily for oneself or bought very cheaply from any reliable supplier of weaving and spinning materials. It is not impossible to spin yarn on a straight peeled twig of ash or hazel stuck through a lump of clay; one can even use a knitting needle stuck through half a potato, but such makeshifts are not to be recommended when well-made spindles can be bought so cheaply.

In addition to a spindle and, of course, some fleece, a small quantity of good, light oil is needed in an oil-can, or in a bottle with a small hole bored through its cork. Olive is the best and pleasantest oil for the purpose.

From *Diagram 7* it will be seen that a spindle consists of a tapered stick, knotched at the top like a crochet hook, with a circular whorl at the bottom; this should not be too heavy – not more than 1 oz. – and it should slip on and off easily.

N.B. *In all the diagrams illustrating spinning, the hands are sketched from the spinner's, not from the onlooker's, point of view.*

1. TEASING. Take a small handful of the poorer part of your fleece, preferably not less than 3 in. in staple. Pull the locks lightly but firmly apart (not roughly enough to break the fibres), so that straw, seeds, dead insects, and so on, fall out. Continue this process until you have a soft, downy mass of wool occupying considerably more space than the original handful. Sprinkle on a few drops of oil and continue to tease the cloudy mass until it is all equally soft and airy with no dense patches.

2. STARTING. Tie about a yard of the hairiest woollen yarn you can

find to the spindle as in *Diagram 8*. Take a small handful of the teased wool in the left hand and the yarn (with the spindle dangling from it) in the right hand between the finger and thumb. Allow about 9 in. of this yarn to lie over the wool in the left hand as in *Diagram 9* and with the right hand draw out a few fibres to wrap round it as shown.

3. PUTTING IN TWIST. Close left finger and thumb firmly on the wool and yarn, a little above the drawn out fibres, and twist the spindle in a clockwise direction between right finger and thumb. As it spins, you will see that the yarn and the fibres twist together and that this twist is prevented from running up into the mass of wool by the pressure of the left thumb on the finger.

4. DRAWING OUT FIBRES. While the spindle is still revolving clock-wise – make sure that it does not reverse – move finger and thumb of the right hand up to within about $\frac{1}{2}$ in. of the left and close them on yarn and fibres as in *Diagram 10*. Immediately release pressure of left thumb just sufficiently to allow about 2 in. of the yarn and a few more fibres to pass down as you draw the left hand upward away from the right (*Diagram 11*).

5. RELEASING TWIST. Close left thumb on finger, release right thumb to allow twist from the still revolving spindle to run up the newly drawn out yarn and fibres.

Repeat stages 4 and 5 until all the rough yarn has been passed down and spun with fibres, by which time the fibres will be themselves making a yarn. The spinners' art consists in drawing out, with one hand, enough fibres from the mass of wool to make the yarn and in knowing when, and how much, to release twist from the other hand so that it will travel up to make a strong yarn. All the time the spindle must be kept revolving in the correct direction.

Do not become discouraged if at first you cannot succeed in making a continuous yarn. No doubt, the spindle will fall to the ground many times because, while concentrating on hand movements, you fail to notice that it is turning in the opposite direction, thus UNSPINNING what you have laboriously spun! When this happens, lay the broken yarn end across the wool in the left hand, using it, as you did the first length of yarn, to start again. While you are learning, you will need at

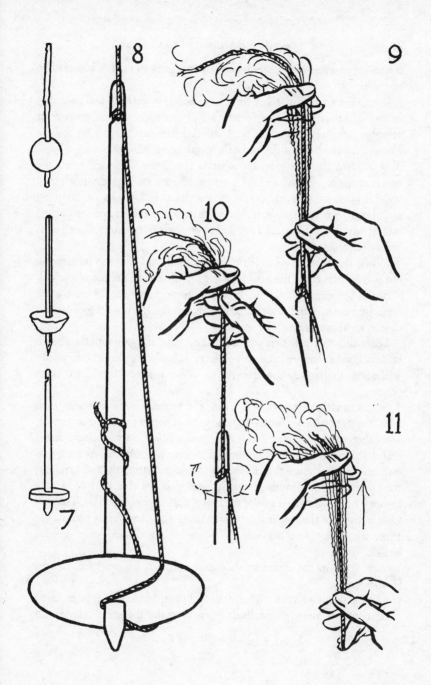

least 6 in. to wrap with fibres when starting, later an inch or two will be enough.

Even when you do at last make a continuous yarn, it will probably be full of kinks and lumps; persevere, nevertheless, and after an hour of apparently hopeless effort, you will suddenly find that your spindle has reached the floor at the end of a length of yarn.

6. WINDING ON. To wind on what is spun, slip the yarn from the notch at the top of the spindle, remove it from under the whorl, then wind it cross-wise up and down the spindle as in *Diagram 12*, allowing each layer to come a little higher so that, when full, it will be packed into a neat cone (*Diagram 12a*). Leave enough unwound to hitch it as before (*Diagram 8*).

7. When the handful of fleece is nearly used, add more to it, drawing out some fibres from the new supply to mingle with the last of the old.

In this preliminary exercise, it is more important to make the correct hand movements and understand the reason for them than to take any care at all about evenness of spinning.

Learn first to know that you *can* make a yarn and you will then begin to watch what happens. Until you have gained confidence, everything will seem to happen too quickly to allow time to think, let alone watch!

8. INCREASING THE DRAFT. Once the spindle is set spinning, each hand has its particular work – the one to hold the twist until it is wanted, the other to draw away – releasing some fibres only. Practise stages 4 and 5 until these actions become quite easy and natural. At first, you will fear to draw more than an inch or so before letting the twist run up; try to increase the length gradually until you are able to draw 4 or 5 inches – the longer the staple of the fleece, the easier this will be. You will soon notice that the longer the draw or DRAFT, the less tightly twisted the yarn, since the same number of twists are distributed on a greater length.

Yarn spun in the direction described above is known as Z-twisted (*Diagram 13*).

9. REVERSING THE SPIN. When you feel complete confidence in using your hands as already described, learn to make the same movements

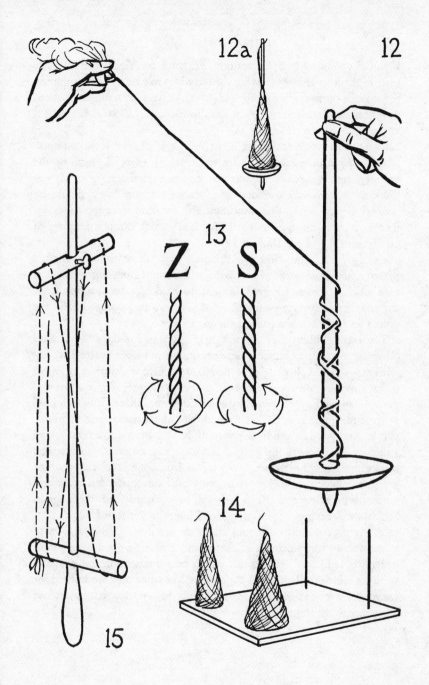

12a

12

Z 13 S

14

15

with the opposite hands, i.e. reading 'left hand' for 'right hand' and *vice versa* in the instructions, viewing the drawings in a mirror, and spinning the spindle anti-clockwise instead of clockwise. Practise until both directions are equally easy. Yarn spun in the anti-clockwise direction is known as S-twisted (*Diagram 13*).

10. EMPTYING THE SPINDLE. If the spindle is allowed to become too full, its weight may cause the yarn to break. To empty it, push up the whorl, so removing the compact cone of yarn. Even though you may not think your preliminary efforts good enough to use, they should be skeined for practice in that important art. To wind from the cone, slip it on to a stand made from a knitting needle stuck through a square of card or thin ply-wood (*Diagram 14*).

11. SKEINING. The simplest skeining equipment is the NIDDY NODDY, the reason for which name will become apparent when it is used quickly. It is not very difficult to make or can be obtained from any supplier of weaving equipment. It is shown in *Diagram 15* and the dotted line indicates the path of the yarn when skeining.

The most efficient way of making good skeins is on a Wrap Reel (*Diagram 16*), a rather difficult piece of equipment for the amateur woodworker to tackle. It should be designed to give a diameter of some definite measurement, e.g. $1\frac{1}{2}$ yards, so that the length of yarn contained in the skein can be determined by counting the number of turns required to wind it. In winding, the skein should not be allowed to pile up in one part of the winder; guide the yarn back and forth to cover the full width of the reel. If this rule is not carefully observed, the tension throughout the whole skein will vary and the long loose loops which will appear when the skein is removed will cause a great deal of trouble when dyeing the yarn. Wrap reels can be obtained from the London School of Weaving, 136, Kensington Church Street, London.

12. TYING THE SKEIN. Having taken the trouble to spin yarn, learn to tie it in a proper manner so that it will remain in good order while being scoured, dyed, etc. Skeins which come undone in the dyebath, skeins of which the beginning and end are lost when they are wanted for use, skeins with so few ties that they cannot be properly shaken out, are a disgrace to the spinner who made them.

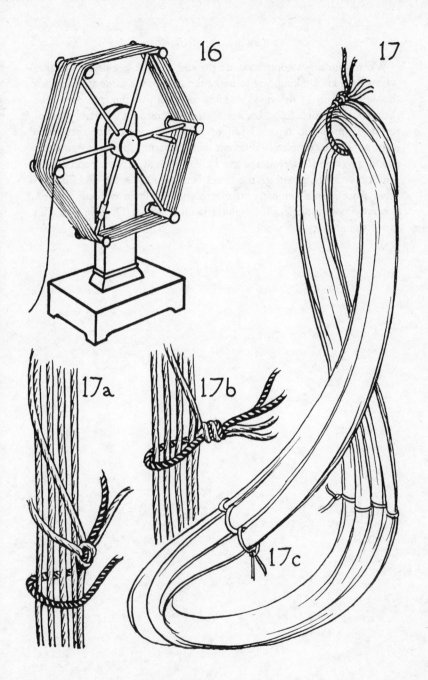

16  17

17a  17b  17c

When winding is completed, tie the end and the beginning together with a firm knot taking care to make the tension the same as the rest of the skein. (Do NOT tie one loose knot and then pass the ends round the skein to tie a double knot, because either the tension is inevitably lost or the tie is made too tightly.) Leave ends of 2–3 in. and to these tie a length of some completely different undyed yarn, sufficient to go easily round the skein (*Diagrams 17a* and *b*). If it is tight, scouring and dyeing solution will not penetrate the fibres beneath it. Tie the skein in two other places, equally loosely; if silk, cotton, or linen is being skeined, these two ties should lace through the skein as shown (*Diagram 17c*). This is not so necessary for wool.

*Chapter Five*

# THE ART OF SPINNING WOOL

THE reader who has handled both long and short wool fleeces will have realized already that the problems encountered in spinning them are rather different. The shorter wools need very thorough teasing while the long wool seems to draw out naturally with the fibres lying parallel to one another. The silky character of so many long wools shows to the best advantage when it is drafted in this way. From comparatively early times, the two distinct methods have been practised and because the long lustrous wools were used in that district, the name of the town of Worstead became associated with a particular method of spinning, the yarn which resulted and also the material made from it.

To-day, WORSTED and WOOLLEN are terms used to describe the two quite different methods of spinning wool. Some handspinners draw no hard and fast line between the two and spin the particular wool they happen to be using in the way which seems best suited to it, which is all to the good, but if handspinning is to assist us to understand commercial yarns, it is advisable to practise each method deliberately.

## *WOOLLEN SPINNING*

From the preliminary experiments suggested in the previous chapter, the reader will have come to understand that the production of an even, well-controlled yarn depends on the smooth regularity with which it can be drawn out. However carefully he may have teased the fleece, he will have encountered awkward lumps and little tufts which interfere with any attempts to keep an even flow. Regularity can only be obtained by a further teasing process which is called CARDING because the heads of teasel plants (*la cardère* = teasel) were used for the purpose until they were superseded by carding cloth made of leather or heavy material inset with fine wire hooks. The cloth is mounted on a pair of wooden bats with handles called CARDERS, obtainable from all good suppliers of spinning equipment, and as carding is quite hard work, care should be taken to choose carders with comfortably rounded handles set smoothly into the back of the cards.

## CARDING

Mark your carders clearly on the back, L for left hand and R for right hand, and use them always in this way. They are, of course, both the same when new, but they soon acquire characteristics which make them unpleasant to use in the opposite hands.

1. Choose some of your better wool, if possible not longer than 3 in. in staple, and tease it out thoroughly as described in *Chapter Four, par. 1.*
2. Sit firmly on an ordinary chair with the left heel and toe squarely on the ground and the right knee slightly bent so that the ball of the foot rests on the ground just under the chair. Rest card L on the left knee with the handle, firmly grasped in the left hand, pointing to the left and slightly away from you. With the right hand lay a small piece of the teased wool on to the card by catching the fleece into hooks about $\frac{1}{2}$ in. from the top at the side nearest your body, stretching the fibres down with a drawing motion so that the whole piece is attached to the hooks from top to bottom of the card (*Diagram 18*). Spread another piece on beside the first in the same way and continue thus until the surface of the card is covered by a *thin* layer of wool.
3. Take card R in the right hand (*Diagram 19*), and draw it lightly but firmly across card L with the movement indicated in the diagram. Repeat this two or three times rather more firmly. Most of the wool will now be on card R.
4. Transfer the wool to card L by standing R on it as in *Diagram 20*, moving R steadily down L as indicated; the layer of fleece will be left behind.
5. Repeat Stage 3.
6. Transfer the wool to R by resting the card R on the right knee, placing L on it as in *Diagram 21* and moving it steadily down as indicated; this leaves the layer of wool on R.
7. Again repeat Stage 3.

Continue this rhythm – brush, transfer wool to L; brush, transfer wool to R; brush, transfer to L; brush, transfer to R, etc., ending with – brush, transfer to L – until the fleece lies evenly spread in a thin film on card L with a delicate fringe of fibres hanging from the bottom edge

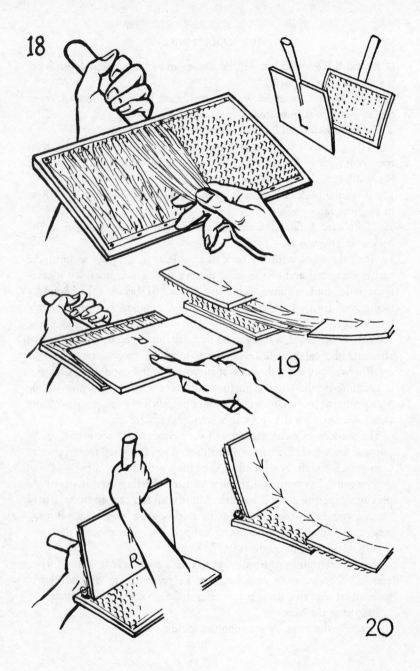

of the card. How many times the actions must be repeated depends on the character of the fleece.

8. Hold the cards as in *Diagram 22* and brush R steadily down L from top to bottom as indicated.

9. Transfer wool from L to R (see Stage 6) very lightly.

10. Transfer wool from R to L (see Stage 4) even more lightly, then transfer it back to R very lightly indeed so that it rests on the surface of R slightly curled as in *Diagram 23*.

11. With the back of L, curl it up in a roll towards the handle of R as in *Diagram 24*.

12. Turn card L face downwards and tip the curling wool on to the back as in *Diagram 25*.

13. Roll the wool with the back of card R as in *Diagram 26* until the curl is elongated and of the same density throughout, then lay it carefully aside until required. This is a ROLAG (*Diagram 27*). A goodly number of rolags should be made so that spinning can proceed uninterrupted.

Made as described, a rolag is, so to speak, air rolled in wool. We can attenuate the rolag, still keeping this tube-like construction, but the result is without strength unless it is twisted at the same time. Our aim in spinning by the woollen method is to retain as nearly as possible the high proportion of air to wool, putting in sufficient twist – but no more than sufficient – for the amount of strength required.

The amount of twist needed will vary enormously according to the purpose for which the yarn will be used. Yarn for warp requires more than yarn for weft. A yarn to be used for a soft scarf or a baby's shawl will be much less twisted than yarn for hard-wearing dress material. As previous experiments will have shown, it is all too easy to make a hard twisted yarn but it takes long practice to produce a wool which is light, airy, and at the same time strong enough for use and with the twist evenly distributed through its whole length.

Before attempting to learn how to spin a particular quality of yarn, one more preliminary exercise must be practised. It will be clearly understood that five distinct processes make up the act of spinning:

1. Preparing the fibre.

2. Creating the twist by spinning the spindle.

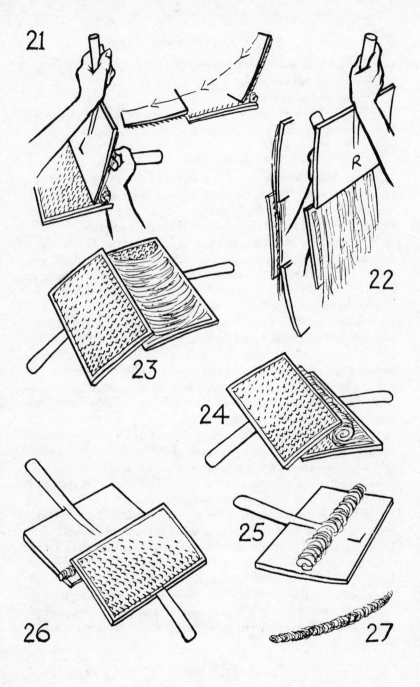

3. Drafting, i.e. drawing out the fibres.

4. Allowing the twist to pass.

5. Winding on the spun yarn.

As described hitherto, each of these actions was performed separately. Now, practice is needed to make numbers 3 and 4 simultaneous.

### SPINNING

14. Take a rolag in the left hand so that it lies over the top of the hand as does the teased wool and yarn in *Diagram 9*. Wrap a few fibres from it round the yarn already on the spindle – this should be Z-twisted since the spindle will be turned clockwise, i.e. in the right hand.

15. Spin the spindle, draw out fibres and allow twist to run up as described in *Chapter Four*, pars. *3, 4* and *5*. If your rolag is well made, you will be able to make a much more even yarn than before. Continue to spin until you are well accustomed to the 'feel' of carded fleece, endeavouring to make the draft as long as possible.

16. Now try to allow some twist to run up *as you draw out*. At first, you will need to open and close the right finger and thumb very quickly and frequently. Many times the spindle will fall because insufficient twist has run up. Persevere until you are able to use the right hand to spin the spindle and to hold the twist back lightly and intermittently, while the left finger and thumb lightly control the rolag by freeing just enough to take the amount of spin which passes up each time from the right hand. It is this light touch with both hands which will give fullness and softness to the yarn; it is by no means easy to achieve, so be prepared to practise, undeterred by many failures.

As explained (in *Chapter Four*) the same actions must be practised with the opposite hands to produce S-twisted yarns.

N.B. It is necessary to learn to use the right hand for drawing, since most people draft with the right hand when spinning on a wheel.

17. SOME DIFFICULTIES – HOW TO AVOID OR OVERCOME THEM

(a) *Yarn very kinked*, the beginner's most common fault. The result of being afraid to draw a sufficient length of fleece and also of making all movements too slowly; usually overcome when confidence grows.

(b) *Broken yarn difficult to join on to rolag.* If at all tightly spun, the end should be teased out and several inches wrapped with fibres and twisted –

in the correct direction – sharply between the finger and thumb.

(c) *Fibres drawing out very unevenly* – sometimes in lumps, sometimes only a few strands. Generally the result of bad carding – i.e. too much fleece used and rolag too big (it should be about the size of the middle finger); alternatively the fleece may have been unevenly spread on the card in the first instance and/or insufficiently carded, resulting in a rolag of uneven density. Bad sorting can also cause uneven spinning.

(d) *Yarn varying very much in thickness.* The thickness is entirely controlled by the relation of the finger and thumb movement of the upper hand to the amount of twist released from below; the greater the amount of rolag freed, the thicker the yarn, and *vice versa*. The *length* of the upward draw also plays a part in controlling the size. Practice alone will give the regularity of rhythm necessary to produce an even yarn.

(e) *Greatly varying amount of twist in different parts of the yarn.* The chief reason for this in the work of beginners is the failure to realize that to distribute twist evenly, tension is necessary. This the spinner should provide as he draws the fibres in the upper hand away from the twist held lower down. When sufficient confidence is achieved to draw and pass the twist simultaneously, the weight of the spindle provides sufficient tension.

18. ANOTHER METHOD. The principle of this method is the same as that already described, but it is not necessary to keep one eye on the spindle and the amount of twist can be controlled more exactly. Spin the spindle with the lower hand, of course keeping the upper hand closed on the rolag. When a fair amount of twist has come into the yarn between the spindle and the rolag, hold the head of the spindle stationary between the little finger and the palm of the hand, with the finger and thumb closed on the twist. Begin drawing out the rolag, at the same time letting the twist up from the lower hand – which continues to hold the spindle stationary. By gradually lowering the lower hand as one draws upward, most of one rolag can be spun by this one operation. A little should be left in the hand to assist in making a perfect join with the new rolag – the last of the old drawing out with the first of the new. Wind on as already described in *Chapter Four* and repeat the process.

N.B. By this method, the weight of the spindle plays no part in the action of drawing and a slight, but definite pull must be exercised by the lower hand to compensate for this lack of tension.

All Down wools and most Mountain wools can be spun by the woollen method. Of course, each breed of wool will present its own problems and must be handled accordingly, both in carding and spinning.

In spreading the wool on the card, for example, very short stapled Down fleece may have a second thin layer spread below the first, the cut ends of the second row just overlapping the tips of the first. Fine Down wools need more carding than coarser fleeces, especially if the carding cloth is coarse – as it often is on modern cards – but the strokes should be lighter and shorter. The longer stapled wools, such as Exmoor Horn or Romney Marsh, and the coarser wools such as Swaledale demand strong sweeping strokes of one card on the other and the really coarse fleece makes for bigger rolags than the fine wools. Thus, quite naturally, the coarse wool will spin the heavier yarn for which it is suited.

Never lose sight of the fact that the main reason for carding is to make a rolag in which the fibres form a hollow tube, the walls of which consist of evenly spaced fibres lying at right angles to the length of the rolag and that good spinning is that which preserves as much of this construction as possible.

Just as the carding rhythms must be adapted to suit the fleece, so must the rhythms of spinning. Wools of medium staple are easier for the beginner to use than the very long wools which require strong, bold handling and a long draft. Welsh, Cheviot, Exmoor Horn, Kerry, Clun, are all good 'beginner's' fleeces. The short, fine wools are much more difficult because they require confident, light, deft handling if they are to yield their best qualities.

For the true Longwool fleeces, the woollen method is difficult and unsuitable, and in any case few of the Longwools possess the felting qualities essential to the making of a good woollen cloth. The Romney Marsh, nowadays usually classed as a Longwool, is a notable exception.

## WORSTED SPINNING

This method is particularly suitable for use with the longer stapled silky wools. In materials woven from worsted spun yarns, the weave stands out clearly and they cannot be finished to give the close-felted quality which one associates with woollen spun materials such as tweeds, blankets and rugs.

All the processes of worsted spinning are designed to ensure that the fibres lie parallel as the twist runs in, making a smooth yarn which is generally firmer and less hairy than a woollen yarn. Almost any type of fleece can be worsted spun, but only the lustrous, long wools give the sleek silkiness associated with worsted at its best.

19. PREPARING THE FLEECE. Take a lock of wool – not less than 4 in. in staple, longer if possible; sprinkle a tiny drop of olive oil into the palm of one hand and roll the lock gently between the two hands to distribute the oil without breaking the lock. Prepare a number of locks in this way.

20. COMBING. Hand combs are not obtainable nowadays, but for the comparatively small quantities used by a handspinner, a dog rake (or dog stripper) or a comb with strong steel teeth can be used. For fine wools, the writer uses an old carder. Clamp the rake, comb or carder to a table as in *Diagrams 28a, b* and *c*, take a prepared lock of wool, and holding it firmly by the cut ends (i.e. NOT by the tips – see page 19, line 23), draw it smartly through the rake, comb or carder. Repeat this several times, then turn it over to comb the under side similarly (*Diagram 29*). Now take the lock by the tips and repeat the whole process, by which time the short fibres – called NOILS – will be collected in the teeth of the comb. The long fibres – called TOPS – will remain, straightened out and parallel, in the hand.

The noils should be removed from the comb and kept for carding with wool for woollen spinning.

21. SPINNING. Take the combed wool in the left hand as in *Diagram 30*, uniting a few fibres to the yarn on the spindle in the usual way. Turn the spindle clockwise and begin drawing out a few fibres, partly with the right hand and partly by drawing the left hand away from the right. The fibres drawn out must lie fanwise across the left forefinger, with the weight of the spinning spindle on them, while the right forefinger and thumb slide up them, smoothing the yarn as the twist runs up (*Diagram 31*).

Simply, the rhythm is this: draw, with LEFT finger and thumb *nearly* closed, right finger and thumb closed; stroke upwards with RIGHT finger and thumb *nearly* closed, left finger and thumb closed.

Make sure that the spindle keeps revolving and aim at keeping the fibres spread neatly fanwise and fully tensioned; *both* hands move away from each other when drawing. The length of draw will depend on the length of staple; it need be seldom more than an inch or two. The yarn should be smooth, even and as fine as the wool allows; once again, the amount of twist must depend on the purpose for which the yarn is required, and should be no more than necessary.

In all spinning, whether by the woollen or the worsted method, the thickness or 'count'* of the yarn should be directly governed by the character of the fleece and the purpose for which the yarn will be used. Fine wools should be used for fine yarns; it is only justifiable to use them for thick yarns if they are soft and lightly spun. The noils from worsted spinning can be mixed with other wool and carded for woollen spinning, and provided that care is taken to obtain even mixing, no part of a fleece need be wasted.

The handweaver, working for the first time with fleece of an unfamiliar breed, is strongly advised to make experimental spinnings, to weave them and, above all, to finish them, before embarking on a complete piece of work. Some types of fleece need more twist than others to give the same degree of strength and the most suitable type of spin for any particular piece of work can only be decided on the results of the particular trials.

If the yarn is to be scoured and dyed before use for weaving or knitting, the beginner should subject small samples to the same treatment. A yarn which seems quite tightly twisted while 'in the grease' may prove far too delicate to stand up to scouring and dyeing, though it may be quite satisfactory for weaving which will be scoured and dyed in the piece.

Yarns to be used for knitting and worsted spun yarns are usually plied, a subject dealt with in *Chapter Ten*, *Section* A.

* Yarn counts are explained briefly in *Chapter Twelve*.

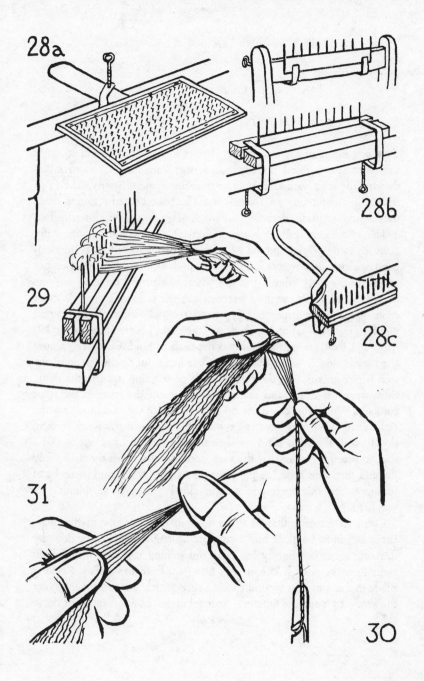

*Chapter Six*

## THE SPINNING WHEEL

THE possession of a spinning wheel does not necessarily add to one's ability to spin a good thread, indeed, there are many who maintain that spindle spun yarns are superior in softness and elasticity. The main advantage of spinning on a wheel is the increased speed resulting from the fact that twisting, drawing and winding go on without interruption.

The spindle, instead of hanging vertical, is suspended horizontally between two uprights and the whorl is made to revolve by a continuous band which passes round it and also round the rim of a much bigger wheel. In the early wheels, this big wheel was turned by hand and one can get an idea of how they were used in the following way. Wind a piece of roughish paper tightly round the polished shaft of a spool winder (*Diagram 54*) and stick down the end. Take a rolag in the left hand and wind enough of it round the shaft to hold. Continue turning the handle slowly while moving the left hand out to the left until the spin begins to run into the rolag instead of winding it on to the shaft; then, open the finger and thumb and draw out the rolag as the twist runs up. When you can draw no further, move the hand towards the right until what you have spun winds on to the shaft. Keep turning slowly with the right hand and again move the left hand out to allow spin to run up. Notice that the yarn does not *all* slip off the shaft, only the end turn slips round as the twist passes up. Of all hand methods of spinning, this one corresponds most closely to machine spinning of woollens.

One can imagine that in order to spin continuously in this way, the rolags must be made into a continuous length. This can be done by drawing them out lightly by hand and joining together with a light twist to make what is known as a ROVING. In former times, a roving made in this way was wound round a stick which was either held under the arm – by a spindle spinner – or fixed into a stand on the floor or, in later wheels, into a fitting designed for it. This stick is the DISTAFF.

The fully developed treadle spinning wheel, usually called the Brunswick wheel, is a very simple piece of mechanism by modern standards. The feature which was such an immense step forward from the earlier wheel was the clever mechanism which winds on the yarn as it is spun. The credit for this invention has always been given to a woodworker of Wattenburg named Jürgen, but students of the drawings of Leonardo da Vinci have long been familiar with a carefully worked-out sketch showing not only a 'flyer', but also an arrangement for dispensing with the guide hooks by methods incorporated into spinning machinery hundreds of years later. This drawing was shown in the Leonardo da Vinci Quincentenary Exhibition in London in 1952.

The wheels shown in *Diagrams 32* and *33* are the types in most common use to-day; the tiny sketches show some not unusual variants. The traditional names for the various parts are delightful, those known to the writer being given in the diagrams.

Although apparently so simple in construction, the action of the spinning wheel is extremely subtle and, to make it function really well, a thorough understanding and a nice adjustment of all its parts is essential. Before attempting to spin, the reader should study the following paragraphs with the greatest care and carry out the suggested experiments, several times if necessary, until complete familiarity with all the adjustments is attained. It is useless to try to learn all about the wheel and also how to handle the wool at one and the same time.

1. YOUR OWN WHEEL. Study this carefully with the two diagrams before you, identifying its component parts. If it has no driving band, put one on. Ordinary string is NOT suitable; strong, not too smooth cotton yarn or hard twisted woollen cord will work well. First of all, set the tension screw about half-way, then pass the band round the rim of the WHEEL, over the BOBBIN WHORL, again round the wheel, then round the SPINDLE WHORL (this has two grooves, ignore the front one at present). Draw the band moderately tight and SEW the ends together. Adjust the TENSION SCREW until the band is *just not* taut.

2. TREADLING. Sit on an ordinary chair with the wheel in such a

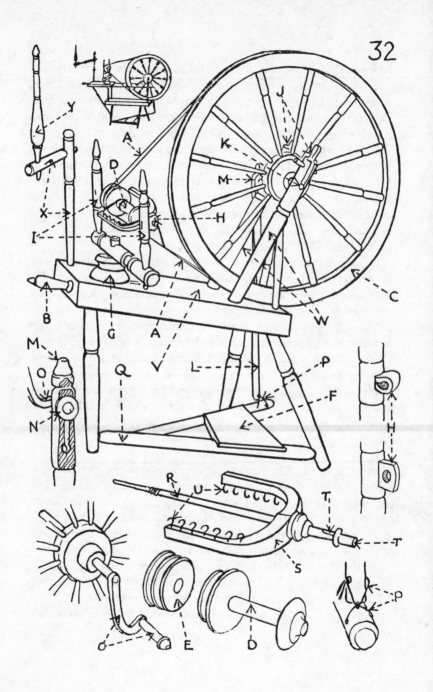

A. Driving band.

B. Tension screw.

C. Wheel.

D. Bobbin.

E. Spindle whorl or wharve.

F. Treadle.

G. Mother-of-all.

H. Leather bearings.

I. Maidens.

J. Wheel pegs or wedges.

K. Axle bearings.

L. Footman.

M. Head of footman.

N. Washer.

O. Axle crank.

P. Treadle cord.

Q. Treadle-bar.

R. Spindle shaft.

S. Flyer.

T. Orifice or eye.

U. Guide hooks.

V. Table.

W. Uprights.

X. Distaff holder.

Y. Distaff.

Z. Lantern distaff.

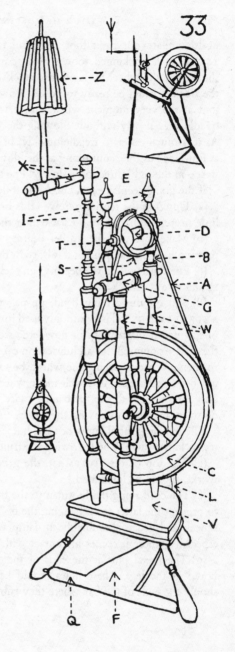

33

position that your right foot, heel and toe, rests comfortably on the TREADLE; a stockinged foot is more comfortable than a high-heeled shoe. Start the wheel by hand in a clockwise direction and as you feel the treadle rising, be ready to press it down lightly with the ball of the foot at the very moment when you feel it *wants* to descend. Aim to treadle very slowly without allowing the wheel to reverse its direction. As it is much easier to treadle quickly, begin quickly, then slow down as much as possible, continuing at this slow, even pace. Stop, and try to start – in the right direction – slowly. Practise until you can do this.

If the going seems heavy, check the following points in this order:

(a) Unscrew the tension screw – this brings the MOTHER-OF-ALL a little nearer to the wheel, so slackening the band slightly.

(b) Make sure that the leather bearing on the front MAIDEN is not pressing hard on the spindle; if it is, twist the maiden slightly in its socket.

(c) Put a little oil on the bearings on each maiden (this should be done in any case).

(d) Slip off the driving band, un-peg the wheel, and lubricate the AXLE BEARINGS; oil is commonly used for this but graphite, in the form of soft pencil sharpenings or powdered stove blacklead, is preferable, in the writer's opinion, for all lubrication *except* the leather bearings on the maidens. When replacing the wheel, be sure the wedges and pegs have not been exchanged; in a well-made wheel, every part fits in one place only! Remember to slip the band – twice – round the wheel; failure to do so means again removing the wheel.

The treadling should now be easy, but if groans and squeaks are heard, try to locate them. The following are fruitful places to search:

(e) The top of the FOOTMAN, the groove in which the axle crank works, should be lubricated.

(f) The cord tying the footman to the treadle should be tight enough to prevent the latter from banging the floor. If linen cord is used, it can squeak and groan abominably in damp weather. Rub vaseline into it, especially where it comes in contact with the wood.

(g) The metal pins at the ends of the TREADLE-BAR fit into holes bored in the legs. These holes should be lubricated with graphite as should the ends of the bar where they rub the legs.

The wheel should now run very sweetly and only one thing more is likely to need attention, namely the SPINDLE SHAFT. Twist the front maiden and thus release the BOBBIN and FLYER; to remove the bobbin, the spindle whorl must be unscrewed. In modern wheels the screw is left-handed, i.e. twist *clockwise* to unscrew; in old wheels the whorl is sometimes forced on and sometimes has a square hole which fits to a similarly shaped place on the spindle. The metal shaft of the spindle should be clean and smooth; if your wheel is old, it may be rusty and sticky with old wool grease. Clean off the rust with very fine emery paper and polish the spindle with metal polish; at the same time see that the hole through the bobbin is clear and clean. Replace all the parts, not forgetting to pass the two rounds of the driving band over the spindle whorl and the bobbin whorl when replacing the flyer in the bearings (*Diagram 32A*).

3. LEARNING TO USE THE WHEEL. Paradoxically, the easiest way to learn how a spinning wheel works is not to spin, but to ply two spun yarns together. Wind two balls of cotton or woollen yarn – 3-ply knitting yarn unravelled from an old garment will serve admirably – and put each one in a separate jam jar. (If you have wound spools, put them on a spool rack.) Tie about a yard of any yarn, not string, tightly round the bobbin shaft, bring it over the guide hooks and out through the orifice with the threading hook or with a bent hair pin as in *Diagram 34*. Put the balls of wool at your left and *tie* the two ends to the yarn hanging from the orifice. Treadle slowly – wheel turning clockwise – as described above and you will see that the yarn on the bobbin begins to wind on – also clockwise. Help the knot through the orifice and over the guide hooks and when it is wound on to the bobbin, stop!

*Experiment (a).* Of the two grooves on the spindle whorl to which reference has already been made (see *par. 1, page 59*), one is deeper than the other, thus giving two rims of differing size in which the driving band can run. The deeper groove, i.e. the smaller diameter, is usually that nearer the bobbin. Slip the band on to the larger one. Take the two woollen yarns between the finger and thumb of the left hand as if for spinning, begin treadling slowly and allow the yarns to pass quite freely into the orifice. You will see that, at the same time as they are being wound on to the bobbin, they are being twisted together; take note of the amount of twist, then close your finger and thumb on the yarns and stop treadling. With the right hand, slip the driving band on to the other – smaller – groove of the whorl.

Again treadle slowly, allowing the yarns to pass freely, and you will see that, while the speed at which they are wound on remains the same, the amount of twist is increased.

The use of these two grooves provides one method of controlling the amount of twist. Some spinners say that the larger diameter was traditionally used for weft which is lightly spun, while the smaller diameter was used for the tighter spun warp yarns.

*Experiment (b).* Replace the driving band on the larger diameter and screw up the tension screw to tighten the driving band a little. Treadle and allow the yarns to pass freely as before, taking note of the rate at which they are drawn in to wind on, then close finger and thumb on the yarn and stop treadling. With the right hand, slacken the driving band (by unscrewing the tension screw – if too slack the wheel alone will revolve).

Again treadle slowly, allowing the yarns to pass freely, and you will feel that they are being drawn in and wound on more slowly with the amount of twist remaining much the same; it will appear to be much greater because it is distributed over a shorter length of the yarns.

The rate of winding on can be controlled by the use of the tension screw.

*Experiment (c).* Set the tension to make the driving band just *not* taut and set the front maiden in its socket so that the leather bearing is exactly at right angles to the spindle shaft, i.e. neither pressed closely against it nor turned away from it.

Treadle slowly and allow the yarns to pass freely and note the amount of twist and the rate of drawing in to wind. Now turn the maiden so that the leather presses a little on the spindle end and note what difference there is in both twist and rate of winding. Turn the maiden still more and again note the difference this makes. Both amount of spin and rate of draw are reduced and if the pressure against the spindle is too great it is impossible to spin at all. For a beginner or when doing some very deliberate piece of work, this minor adjustment is quite useful. On one wheel belonging to the writer the rate of spin can be slightly reduced by this adjustment while the winding rate is unaffected.

The character of yarn can be controlled very accurately by means of these various adjustments. The adjustments in Experiments (a) and (b) assist in controlling the amount of twist in the yarn, (a) directly and (b) by the fact that the greater or lesser length of yarn wound on will have the same number of twists.

N.B. As the bobbin fills, its weight retards its speed, and more than compensates for the increasing size in diameter as the yarn winds on. The ratio of wind-on to twist can be maintained by slight, but regular increases in the tension of the driving band – less than a half-turn of the screw at a time. *When a bobbin is quite empty, the beginner is advised to work with a very slack tension until a few rounds have covered it.*

4. SPINNING WOOLLEN YARN – STARTING. Prepare rolags as before and remove the experimental yarn from the bobbin, leaving the starting piece tied to the bobbin shaft. Pass this over the furthest hook and out through the orifice, but this time fibres from the rolag must be drawn out and spun, not tied, to the yarn.

Hold the rolag in the right hand as in *Diagram 35a.* With the left hand, draw from it a few fibres and twist them clockwise with finger and thumb round an inch or so of the end of the yarn hanging from the orifice.

N.B. The beginner should have a length of at least 12 in. hanging out; the experienced spinner will need only an inch or so.

Begin treadling slowly, holding the fibres twisted on the yarn with the left hand and allowing both hands to move towards the orifice as the starting yarn winds on.

When the left hand, holding the yarn and fibres, comes within a few inches of the orifice, keep both hands still for a second with the left thumb and finger closed. This allows some twist to accumulate between your hand and the point where the yarn passes over the hooks, and you will feel a slight pull. Now, begin drawing out the rolag with the right hand and *at the same time* release the twist with the left hand. The right hand should keep the roving taut while the twist is running up and then it should be carried quickly towards the orifice as the finished yarn winds on.

If the speed of winding takes the yarn into the orifice too quickly for your inexperience to cope with, slacken the tension screw. As soon as you have gained a little confidence you should dispense with this very slack tension which will give an over-spun and kinked yarn.

Meantime, one *must* gain confidence, if necessary by practising this beginning over and over again until the fibres join to the yarn and the twist runs properly into the roving.

Treadling must continue absolutely regularly all the time.

5. SPINNING. The method of controlling the rolag is similar to that described in *Chapter Five, par. 18*, except for the fact that the right hand moves away towards the right instead of upwards (*Diagrams 35 and 35a and b*).

The left hand is held directly in front of and about 1 in. away from the orifice all the time. Treadling should be a continuous steady 'four beats to the bar' all the time and the hand movements are as follows:

Hands close together, left thumb firmly closed on spun yarn close to orifice.

Right hand holding rolag lightly – no twist as yet between right and left hands.

Keep hands in this position for a second or two while twist accumulates between left hand and wheel – do not allow yarn to be drawn in at this stage.

Now release the twist from the left hand and at the same time begin drawing the rolag with the right hand; there must be a definite pull on the growing yarn as the twist runs up, exercised partly by the pull of the wheel, partly by the constant opening and closing of the left finger and thumb to control the twist. The pull while drawing should be sufficient to prevent the yarn from winding on until the right arm is fully out-stretched, i.e. until about a yard of yarn is spun.

Immediately, the left hand frees the yarn and the right hand quickly allows it to wind on, stopping once again about a few inches from the orifice in readiness to repeat the whole process.

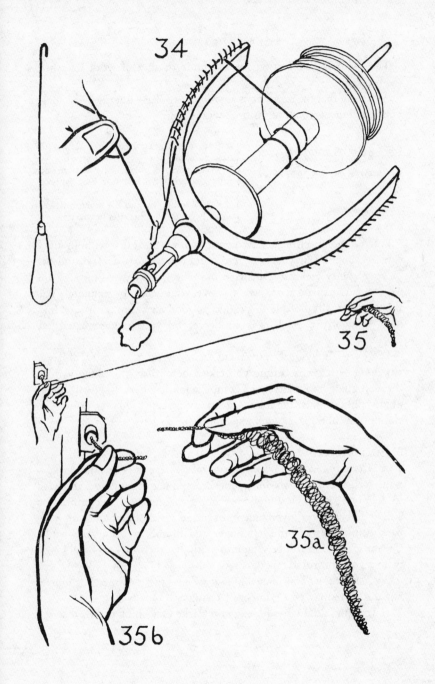

The following suggestion for a definite rhythm of work may help the beginner.

Assuming that the treadling is absolutely regular – as it must be – make your rhythm by counting in time with it thus:

| | |
|---|---|
| *One, two, three, four, five,* | $\left\{\begin{array}{l}\end{array}\right.$ – Both hands near the orifice waiting for twist to come. |
| *six, seven, eight, nine, ten, eleven, twelve, thirteen, fourteen, fifteen,* | $\left\{\begin{array}{l}\end{array}\right.$ – Twist released, rolag being drawn, arm fully extended by fifteenth beat (approx. 1 yard of yarn). |
| *sixteen, seventeen, eighteen,* | $\left\{\begin{array}{l}\end{array}\right.$ – Yarn winding on and the nineteenth beat again becomes the first of a new series. |

Practise and experiment for yourself in this way, at first without much concern about quality, evenness, etc., until you feel reasonable confidence in your ability at least to manage the wheel, then work through the experiments explained in *par. 3* above while actually spinning. You should eventually be able to produce a good airy yarn, coarse or fine, hard or lightly twisted, as your fleece and your requirements may dictate.

Let every individual movement be designed as part of a larger rhythmic pattern. Each time you take a new rolag, move the yarn to the next guide hook; after each complete journey back and forth on the guide hooks, tighten the tension screw by perhaps a quarter or even an eighth turn; nothing should be spasmodic or restless.

6. SOME DIFFICULTIES AND HOW TO OVERCOME THEM.

(a) *The yarn, even the whole unspun rolag disappearing into the orifice* – with such speed that the inexperienced spinner feels almost impelled to follow it in! This purely psychological difficulty is common to almost all beginners; overcome it, once and for all, by holding the yarn back firmly between the left finger and thumb, treadling the while. Of course the yarn will be spun into snarls, but thereafter you will know that you *can* control its rate of entry.

(b) *The yarn not being drawn in to wind on* – the reverse of the above. For this there may be a number of reasons:

*1.* Tension, although adjusted, too slack. One must realize that the driving band will stretch and must be cut and re-set fairly often (see *par. 1, page 59*).

*2.* Yarn too thick or lumpy to pass through the orifice.

*3.* Yarn caught on one of the guide hooks; on an old wheel they may have worn very thin – one may be almost severed.

*4.* A layer of yarn may have wound itself round the spindle shaft between the bobbin and the arc of the flyer.

(c) *The Footman jumping off the crank.* Cut a washer of rubber or metal, fitting it as illustrated in *Diagram 32N*.

(d) *Wheel reversing in direction.* This may indicate insufficient practice in treadling (see *par. 2, page 59*) or the wheel may not be running as freely as it should; without a driving band, the wheel ought to continue revolving on its own fifteen to twenty times after you stop treadling. Check up all the lubrication points.

(e) *Rolag coming to pieces as it is drawn out.* There are several possible causes:

*1.* Waiting for too short a time for twist to accumulate before drawing (*par. 5, page 66*).

*2.* Keeping finger and thumb too much closed on the rolag while drawing.

*3.* Wool unevenly spread on carders and insufficiently carded so that rolag is variable in density.

(f) *Yarn lumpy and uneven.* This is almost invariably the result of careless carding, particularly when rolags are too big. It is difficult to spin really well from rolags much thicker than one's middle finger: it is equally difficult to *make* them really well any bigger than this, unless from very coarse fleece.

7. S AND Z TWISTS. When spinning on a wheel, the hands are used in the same way for either S- or Z-twisted yarns, but the wheel is made to turn anti-clockwise for S yarns and the bobbin will also wind in the reverse direction.

8. LEFT AND RIGHT HANDED SPINNERS. The use of the right hand for drawing is usually accepted as the correct method; it is certainly most suited to the way in which the wheel is designed, but while a left handed draw may look a little awkward, some spinners work in this way with

greater ease, drawing away to the left and almost up to shoulder height.

9. WORSTED SPINNING. This is rather easier on the wheel than on the spindle because the steady 'draw' of the wheel itself enforces a regular, and therefore even, rate of draft.

Set the tension screw to give a moderately fast winding rate (this will be a matter of trial and error; too strong a 'draw' will give a weak yarn, too little will make it hard and over-spun).

Start treadling slowly, hold the combed wool in the left hand and the yarn from the orifice in the right and with the right hand draw out fibres to twist on to it.

When the join is made, spin with the left hand stationary about 6 in. in front of the orifice; the right hand works between them, drawing out the fibres to lie fan-wise over the forefinger of the left hand (Chapter Five, par. 21 and Diagram 31).

The necessary tension as the twist runs up the fan of fibres is provided partly by the gentle draw from the wheel as the yarn winds on, and partly by the stationary left hand.

The ideal rhythm comes when the treadle 'beat' and the draw with the right hand coincide. By careful use of the adjustments possible on a well-designed wheel, one can obtain a very exact control of the character of spin suited to the fleece.

10. SKEINING FROM THE BOBBIN. While it is advisable to remove the bobbin to a spool rack when skeining off the spun yarn, it can be done directly from the wheel.

Allow the wheel to come to rest naturally, slacken the tension, unthread the yarn from the orifice and the guide hooks and turn the flyer into such a position that there will be no danger of the yarn catching in the hooks as it unwinds. Always leave the 'starting yarn' tied to the bobbin spindle for the next lot of spinning.

11. 'SCOTCH TENSION'. Some spinning wheels, particularly old ones of the upright type, have no tension screw and the old Scottish woollen spinners overcame this in the following ingenious way:

The driving band passed round the wheel and thence round the spindle whorl only, not round the bobbin whorl. As the flyer revolved, the bobbin on the same shaft naturally revolved at the same speed so

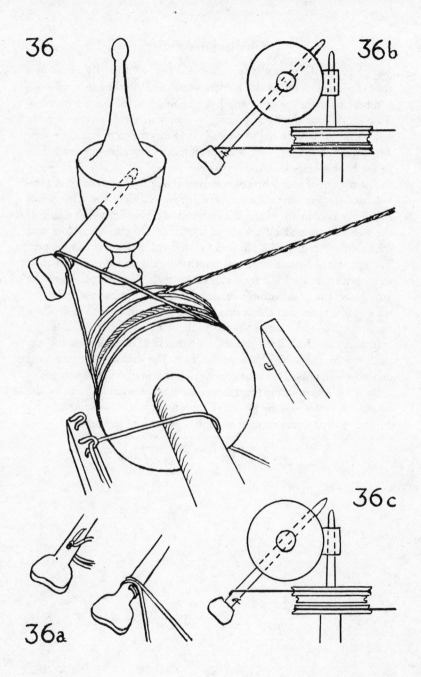

36

36b

36c

36a

that although the yarn was spun, it could not wind on. By means of a thin cord, passed round the bobbin whorl and attached to some convenient part of the spinning wheel, the bobbin was still further retarded. This meant that the flyer, putting in the spin, revolved considerably faster than the bobbin and so wound the spun yarn on to it in the *reverse direction*; i.e. when the wheel was running clockwise, the yarn wound on to the bobbin anti-clockwise and *vice versa*.

The tension of such a brake-cord must be adjusted to a nicety. A convenient arrangement is shown in *Diagram 36*. Here the cord passes round the bobbin whorl and the two ends are passed through a hole in the peg and secured by a knot as shown in *Diagram 36a*. Note that sufficient length of cord is allowed to wind at least once round the peg. The amount of tension needed is surprisingly slight; if the cord is at all tight, neither bobbin nor flyer will move at all. *Diagram 36b* shows the arrangement in plan with the driving band on the spindle whorl only; it should be noted that the position of the peg must be such as to allow the brake cord to be at right angles to the spindle and bobbin shafts.

In many old Irish linen wheels, the same kind of brake control was used, not on the bobbin, but on the flyer. The driving band was used on the bobbin only. This arrangement is shown in plan in *Diagram 36c*.

By a slight turn of the peg the relative rates of wind and spin can be adjusted as perfectly as by the use of the tension screw and spinners who are accustomed to this method of control prefer it to any other.

*Chapter Seven*

## ON BUYING A SPINNING WHEEL

SOONER or later, everyone who has enjoyed spindle spinning wants to possess a spinning wheel and if any quantity of work is contemplated, a wheel is almost essential from the point of view of saving time alone. A well-made example, ancient or modern, will grace any home; the difficulty is that having acquired one specimen, most spinners succumb to the temptation to become collectors.

How and what should one buy? The modern wheel or an old one? To a beginner, the answer would be: 'Neither! If you have the chance to buy a second-hand pre-war wheel of a good make, do so!' However, such an opportunity may not come and since old wheels can be very 'difficult', the spinner without experience will be wise, on the whole, to decide on a new wheel. Seek the advice of a knowledgeable spinner if possible, if not, go to a firm with a highly respected reputation and put yourself in their hands but *never* buy a wheel you have not seen.

The next choice confronting you is between the upright and the horizontal wheel. Considerations of floor space may force you to choose the upright type; its disadvantages are the result of the comparative smallness of the wheel which necessitates quicker treadling and makes production slower. In most respects a well-designed horizontal spinning wheel is more generally useful for serious work. Not only does the bigger wheel increase the speed of spinning, it gives smooth, effortless treadling which, in turn, leads to more rhythmic hand movements. On a good wheel, the fine adjustments are easily made and very exact; the tension screw, for example, moving the whole of the mother-of-all instead of only one maiden as in most upright wheels. Of the two most usual designs, that with a horizontal table and with horizontal bars supporting the uprights and the mother-of-all is very convenient when travelling because the wheel can be lifted out and packed between the horizontal bars; it is not quite so attractive in appearance as the other

73

type in which the sloping table makes it possible to have a very big wheel.

It is safe to say that a wheel which is poor in woodcraft is unlikely to be worth buying.

In a well-made wheel, all the parts which remain fixed are pegged with wooden pegs; metal screws are never used. Many of the beautifully made old wheels had very few fixed parts; the treadle and its bar was made in one piece, and legs and uprights dropped into their appointed sockets, all fitting perfectly. The drier, warmer conditions of our modern homes, however, cause shrinkages never foreseen by the old woodworkers; legs tend to fall out and uprights wriggle out of place, unless they are pegged.

Excellent wheels can sometimes be imported from the Scandinavian countries, particularly Sweden, where suitable wood is plentiful and where the traditional crafts of spinning and weaving and the making of equipment are carried on under the paternal eye of a watchful government. At the time of writing, it is still necessary to obtain, from the Board of Trade, a permit to import.

What about buying an old wheel? Here are temptations and pitfalls innumerable!

There is the collector's 'fancy piece' lending old-world charm to the antique dealer's window in that fascinating little holiday town. It probably has no flyer and no pedal, it may even, like one once offered hopefully to the writer, have its wheel *screwed* fast to the uprights! Beautifully though it may be carved, even painted and inlaid with ivory, if you are wise it will not be for you.

There is also the genuine collector's piece. In the eighteenth and early nineteenth centuries, flax spinning was one of the polite accomplishments of ladies of fashion; it was a drawing-room occupation, and many delightfully dainty, highly decorative wheels have survived to command prices out of all proportion to their value as practical spinning wheels. When they can be found, the plainer sturdy work-a-day wheels of the same period, if in reasonable condition, are much less expensive and of much more use to the practical spinner.

Occasionally, a genuine bargain may turn up looking like a wheel and a bundle of sticks. Even if, among them, there is an undamaged flyer and bobbin, if the requisite number of legs and the uprights are present, the chances are that the wheel will be badly strained – it is peculiarly susceptible to damage when not in its place. You must then decide whether the sum which will have to be spent on having it expertly doctored will be offset by the low price asked 'because it is broken'.

The following points are worth considering when examining an ancient specimen with intent to buy:

1. THE FLYER. Unless you have some very special reason for doing so, never buy a wheel with a very badly damaged flyer or without a flyer. It is even more difficult than the wheel to repair and expert knowledge is required to make a new one which will work happily in an old wheel.

Broken or worn guide hooks are easily replaced by small screw hooks of the best obtainable quality (NOT aluminium). Occasionally both sets of hooks are on the same surface of the flyer (instead of the usual arrangement of one set above and the other below) presumably for greater convenience when plying two or more spun yarns (*Chapter Ten, par. A*) or when spinning S-twisted yarn.

If the spindle shaft is bent, it can usually be straightened without much difficulty.

Slight damage to whorls of bobbin and spindle can be repaired with plastic wood.

The wooden arc of the flyer should be in good condition, neither cracked, chipped nor strained in any way.

2. THE WHEEL. The simplest and most likely damage to this is a few broken or missing spokes where the wheel has always been handled for starting. This is not serious, but they should be replaced before the wheel is used.

If the rim is cracked or the joints are strained, the hub is likely to have suffered also and the metal axle crank is probably bent; this again is work for an experienced craftsman.

If the wheel is sound but does not run true – and the slightest wobble will cause untold vexation when spinning – the grooves in the uprights are probably badly worn. In some old wheels these grooves are reinforced with bone or ivory. It is usually possible to true up the grooves by deepening them very slightly, but it must be done with great care and accuracy; it should not be lightly undertaken by an amateur wood-worker.

3. THE MAIDENS. The maidens themselves should be undamaged in the lower parts, chips out of the carved or turned tops matter little to a spinner. Broken or missing leather bearings are easily made and re-placed. They can be either glued in or wedged with thin wooden wedges (*Diagram 32H*).

4. THE MOTHER-OF-ALL. This must obviously be sound; unfortun-ately, it is usually the first part to be seriously attacked by woodworm (*par. 10 below*).

5. LEGS. A missing or broken leg is not very difficult to replace; much care is needed with front legs when setting in the pedal bar.

6. TREADLE AND BAR. It is quite likely that this may be broken or missing but it is not very expensive to repair or replace.

If the only damage is a bent pin at each end of the bar, it can be put right quite easily.

7. FOOTMAN. This may be missing because it has been lost or the wheel may have been used without one. A cord, fastened to the end of the axle crank and tied fairly tightly down to the back of the treadle, takes its place quite well.

8. DISTAFF. If you are interested in flax spinning, you will need a wheel with a distaff. The lantern type is the most convenient (*Diagram 33Z*), but is not essential. Some old linen wheels have a small fitting to hold a water bowl.

9. TENSION SCREW. A great number of the old wheels which come on to the market are of the upright design and many have no tension screw. Some are fitted with a braking device (*Chapter Six, par. 11*) and if not, it is quite easy to devise something on the lines shown in *Diagram 36*. Wheels of the horizontal type usually have a tension screw. Its position generally saves it from undue harm.

10. WOODWORM. This is a very great nuisance; wood which appears from outside to be in good condition may be almost eaten away and will break under the slightest strain; a wheel which has been badly attacked may well be quite useless. A mild attack may be controlled, and to a certain extent cured, by pickling the affected parts in a strong solution of D.D.T. – the whole part must be submerged.

Difficult repairs to a spinning wheel should only be entrusted to a craftsman with the proper traditional knowledge. The local Museum Authorities can sometimes put one in touch with suitable people; many old wheels, too, have been nursed back to useful life in the workshops of the London School of Weaving.

11. SOME DIFFICULTIES IN USING AN OLD WHEEL.

Examine your wheel carefully in the light of *pars. 1* and *2* of *Chapter Six*, and when all is running smoothly and quietly, experiment with a couple of spools of spun yarn as described in *par. 3* of the same chapter.

One of the commonest troubles is that the driving band frequently slips off the wheel. If the rim is in good condition, the difficulty can probably be traced to a wheel wobble. This may be caused by one of the uprights not being absolutely stationary – a horizontal wheel with a very sloping table can give a lot of trouble in this way – or the wheel itself may have been strained. If the uprights are not glued in, try changing them over; if they appear to be similar in shape, they may fit more firmly. A tiny sliver of wood, even a thin fold of paper, may be enough to steady them. If the wheel is at fault, have it dealt with expertly.

Another common difficulty having the same causes is a jerky draw, i.e. the yarn spins and pays on in fits and starts.

One must remember that any wheel which is not in constant use becomes stiff and uncomfortable very quickly. Very careful attention to all the lubrication points will well repay the time spent.

If your wheel is small and delicate in design, use a suitably thin cord for the band, and of course do not try to spin a disproportionately heavy yarn. The size of the yarn any wheel will spin is determined by the size of the orifice and of the guide hooks: for thick rug yarn one must usually have a flyer specially made.

If you learnt to spin on a modern wheel, you may find great difficulty in adjusting tensions of an old one. Sometimes, years of use have worn the spindle whorls so badly that the diameter is decreased so that the amount of spin is always too great. It is possible to build them up with a little plastic wood or to wind round a few layers of a strong, fine linen yarn. If this does not effect a cure, experiment with a braking device as in *Diagram 36*.

One last word to the houseproud – *never* polish the rim of the wheel.

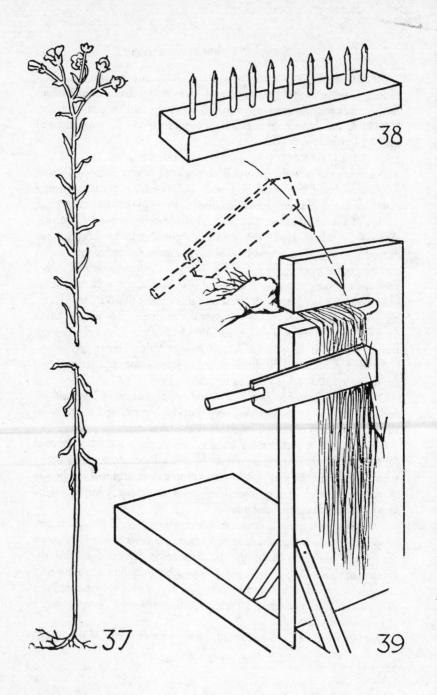

37

38

39

*Chapter Eight*

# FLAX

LINEN yarn is spun from the long inner fibres of the flax plant which remain when the outer straw and the inside pith have been rotted away. It has been used from very early times – evidence of the existence of flax has been found in several excavations of pre-historic sites, and fragments of linen cloth from Egyptian tombs testify to the amazing skill with which the cultivation, preparation and spinning was done as early as 2000 B.C. Flax is frequently mentioned in the Old Testament, and conditions in some areas of the Middle East – in the Nile valley in particular – were undoubtedly favourable to the growing and dressing of the very fine flax which must have been used for some of the surviving fragments of linen.

I. CULTIVATION. Flax (*Linum usitatissimum*), (*Diagram 37*), is a tall, somewhat grain-like plant bearing a blue flower. It is not particularly difficult to grow, but the processes of preparing the fibres from it, to make them suitable for spinning, are long and complicated and the resulting quality of the flax depends almost entirely on how well they are carried out.

A light sandy soil is favourable to fineness of fibre, a heavy clay gives a bigger but coarser crop. The seed is sown in April and the plant takes about a hundred days to come to maturity. It should have one unbranched stem from two to three feet in length and, to encourage this single growth, the seed must be sown thickly and evenly.

When the stem begins to yellow, the leaves to wither and the seeds to turn brown, it is pulled up by the roots, NOT cut, because, through all the stages of preparation, length of fibre is one of the qualities to be preserved. If a handful is grasped just under the point where the seed heads branch, it pulls quite easily. Thin stalks generally denote fine flax fibres and if a small quantity is being dealt with, fine and coarse can be kept separate in this and all the succeeding operations. When gathered and bundled with roots all one way, it is spread to dry out of doors for a few days; the old flax growers used then to store it in a dry place until the following year, considering that this period of maturing improved the quality.

2. RIPPLING. This is the process of removing the seeds and it is done by drawing the upper part of the bundles through a coarse comb called a rippling comb (*Diagram 38*).

3. RETTING. The fibres which will be used for spinning run the whole length of the plant and in order to free them from the rest of the vegetable matter – the outer straw and the inner pith – the latter are rotted away. This can be done by laying the opened out bundles on grass to be exposed to sun, rain, wind and dew, a method known as DEW RETT-ING. It takes a very long time, the flax needs frequent attention to prevent it from ever getting dry, and the fibres become very dark in colour.

An easier method is to lay the bundles in soft clear water in warm weather for ten days to a fortnight; in colder weather much longer is needed because decomposition is slower. Ponds and ditches were frequently used for this, but slowly moving water is preferred because the fibres do not become discoloured by the presence, in large quantities, of the decomposing vegetable matter, so that less severe bleaching is needed at a later stage.

Over-retting is as disastrous as under-retting (*par. 5 below*). To test it, a few stalks should be gently broken a little above the root and if the outer straw breaks away easily, it is ready for the next process.

4. GRASSING. This is done to separate up the flax fibres when the outer straw has rotted. The bundles are untied and the flax is laid out thinly on grass for a few days until it changes colour; it is then turned over and left until the newly exposed sides have also changed colour. Next it is stooked up to dry off, and then taken in to be stacked in a dry place for a few weeks. Quick drying by artificial means spoils the quality, making the flax harsh for spinning.

5. SCUTCHING. The core and what is left of the outer parts of the plant must be broken up and beaten away by scutching. For hand

scutching, a board with a slot in it is used as shown in *Diagram* 39. A handful of flax is held by the root ends in this slot and the fibres are beaten down against the side of the board with a wooden blade as shown. The bundle is twisted round and round during the process and then reversed so that the root ends can receive similar treatment until all the rest of the plant, the BOON, is beaten away. If retting has been incomplete, the heavy scutching required will weaken the flax fibres and cause much waste; the fibres of over-retted flax will also suffer at this stage and will break into short lengths.

6. HACKLING. This is the final process in the dressing of flax. The bundle of flax fibres is held by the root end and combed through a coarse metal-toothed comb to remove remains of boon and short fibres. This must be done several times and if fine flax yarn is wanted, the final hackling is done through a comb with finer teeth. The short mass of fibres hackled out is called TOW, the long strands of flax are called LINE. When a bundle or STREAK (or STRICK) of flax has been sufficiently hackled, all long loose strands are removed to make it tidy for spinning.

Modern flax production is developed from these hand methods. Rippling, scutching and hackling are done by machine and most retting now takes place in artificially warmed water in tanks in large factories. The best flax obtainable to-day comes from Courtrai, in Belgium, but flax which is perfectly satisfactory for the handspinner is obtainable from various sources in the British Isles.

7. PREPARATION OF DRESSED FLAX FOR SPINNING. Well-dressed flax is supplied in a smooth and tidily twisted strick, needing only to be shaken out to loosen the fibres a little. It should be held firmly first near one end and then near the other and given one sharp shake each time. Flax which has not been well dressed is full of short lengths of straw-like stuff, the boon, and if shaking as described will not remove it, the strick, or about 1½ oz. of it, should be hackled with a metal dog comb. Hold the strick firmly in the middle and comb as you would comb out tangles from a young child's hair, beginning near one end and gradually working up to the middle; then turn it round and comb the other end in the same way. Remove any long straggling strands and give it a final shake as

described. The tow left in the comb can be combed again to give short fibres for experiment.

8. EXPERIMENTS ON A SPINDLE. Before learning to spin on the wheel, the reader is urged to gain some knowledge of the handle of flax and of the problems that arise in spinning it. Take in the left hand some of the combed out tow or, if it has not been necessary to hackle it, separate a few fibres from the strick. Hold the fibres in the hand as illustrated in *Diagram 9*, drawing a few fibres out with the right finger and thumb to twist with the yarn from the spindle. Flax can be made to adhere to itself and to other fibres if it is damp, and the right finger and thumb must therefore be kept slightly wet while spinning. The quite unhygenic method of wiping the ball of the thumb on the lower lip is the easiest and makes the best yarn, but most people prefer to have a small bowl of water or a saturated sponge in a dish for this purpose. It must be kept very near the hand. The aim is to draw down enough fibres to make the yarn while allowing no more than sufficient twist to run into them, and to smooth them upward with the damp finger and thumb while the twist is running up. The hand holding the fibres remains stationary, the finger and thumb opening and closing to release or slightly restrain the fibres and to prevent the twist from running into the whole mass. Meanwhile the lower hand moves up and down; down when drawing fibres, up when smoothing the yarn – it must also keep the spindle spinning.

The great difficulty is that the fibres do not draw out easily if they are at all long and that, in the hand, they become drawn up into a tangled bundle; it is for this reason that the shorter fibres should be used when spinning from the hand in this way. The other difficulty is, of course, to keep the yarn smooth and this is achieved mainly by stroking it with the damp finger and thumb.

Although it seems fairly certain that the Ancient Egyptians spun their incredibly fine yarn from the hand, without using a distaff, there is good reason for believing that they made some kind of roving first and spun on to the spindle from this. In Europe, it has been customary, at least from Roman times, to spin flax from a prepared distaff. Before learning to do this, use the spindle, with the left hand drawing down fibres and the right hand holding them, so that the left hand will have some practice in doing the work required of it when spinning on a wheel.

9. DRESSING THE DISTAFF. From the above, you will realize that, for convenient spinning of flax, the fibres *must* be arranged in some way which will allow the long fibres to be drawn out without disarranging and tangling a large quantity of material.

Many old continental spinners, working with very fine flax and having very tall distaffs, tied one end of the strick to the top and having spread the fibres carefully all round the distaff, they tucked up any straggling ends at the bottom, wound and tied a ribbon round, to keep the whole in place, and worked from that. The writer has tried this, but even with flax of finer quality than is obtainable to-day, found it much less pleasant to work from than the method of dressing the distaff usually employed here. This is as follows:

Having shaken out a strick of flax, weigh it and separate from it about $1\frac{1}{2}$ oz. by parting some from the end you have been holding, then pulling it away sharply.

If your distaff has a 'lantern' head (*Diagram 33Z*), so much the better; if not, bunch up some tissue paper and wind it round the distaff lightly to make a cone shape as in *Diagram 40*. Tie it firmly just below the ridge at the top, roll it in another piece of tissue paper and stick this down the edge so that it covers the cone smoothly.

You will need about 2 yards of soft ribbon $\frac{1}{2}$–$\frac{3}{4}$ in. wide, a cloth to spread over your knees and enough string, and to spare, to tie round your waist.

Tie this string firmly to the strick of flax about 3 in. from the end you were holding, sit on an ordinary chair (not an armchair), spread the cloth on your lap and tie the string holding the flax tightly round your waist so that the strick lies down the centre of your lap, as in *Diagram 41*.

Now take the flax in your left hand, as near the far end as you can comfortably reach, and keeping it stretched out, move your left arm over to your right knee. With the right hand stretched out flat, separate a few fibres from the strick and hold them on your right knee with the 'flat' of the right hand as in *Diagram 42*.

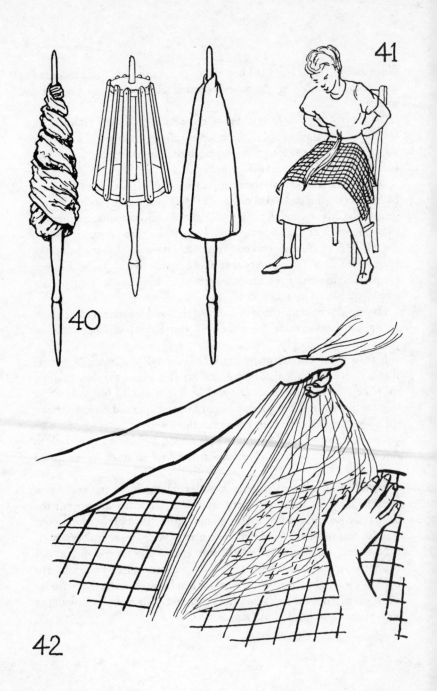

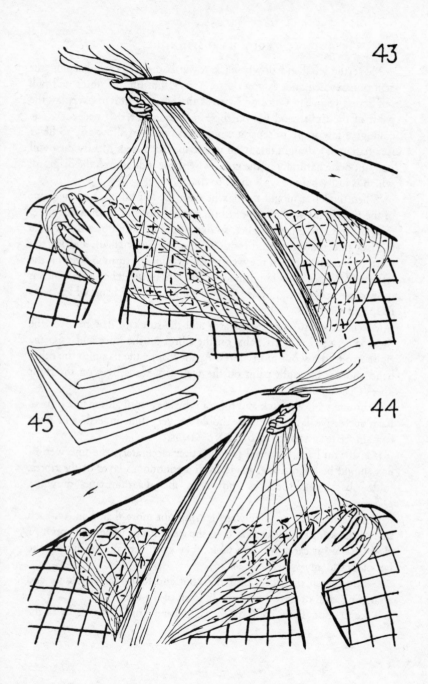

Move the left hand slowly back towards the left knee, keeping the arm outstretched and, as you do so, a very thin film of fibres will pull out across your lap. Once or twice as the left arm moves over, lay the palm of the right hand flat on these spreading fibres. If necessary, encourage a few more to separate, but on no account allow any to lie as if radiating in a straight line from where the flax is tied. Mostly they will pull out quite naturally in the cross-wise shape indicated in the diagram, which is just what we wish them to do.

When the left arm and the flax lie over the left knee, place the palm of the right hand on the film of fibres on the knee and, at the same time, raise the left arm a little higher, so drawing out more fibres. Now take the flax into the right hand (with right arm outstretched), and lay the palm of the left hand on the web of fibres which is turning over on the left knee (*Diagram 43*). This time it is the right outstretched arm which is moved towards the right knee and the palm of the left hand which helps to spread the fibres.

When the right outstretched arm and the strick of flax are over the right knee, place the left palm on the fibres on the knee and raise the right arm to draw out more fibres. Again change the flax into the other hand and use the right palm on the web as it turns over on the right knee (*Diagram 44*).

Continue working back and forth in this way until all the flax is used. Each successive layer of fibres should be very thin indeed, and must contain NO STRAIGHT RADIATING LINES.

N.B. If you have followed the directions accurately, the fine web of flax should be a fan shape, made from a continuous layer of the fibres, folded back and forth as shown in the diagrammatic drawing, *Diagram 45*.

Cut the string from your waist leaving not more than $\frac{1}{2}$ in. on each side of the knot tying the flax, then slip your hands under the apron or cloth and lay it carefully on a table; take great care not to disturb the fan of flax in any way (*Diagram 46*).

Gently loosen the fibres near the knot and fold over any loose and straggling ends of fibre round the bottom of the fan.

Take the distaff and lay it on the right-hand edge of the fan with the

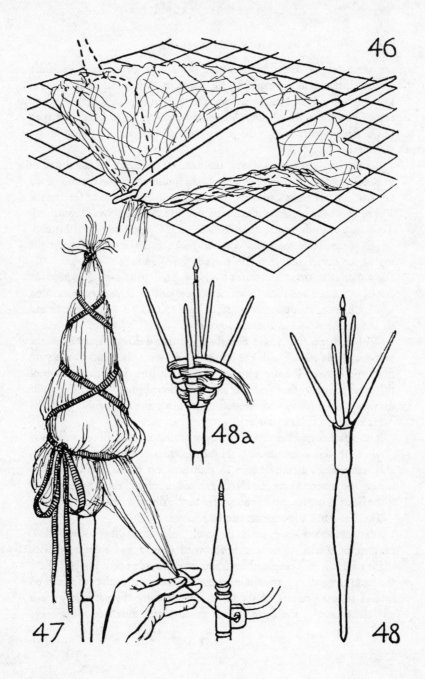

46

47

48a

48

top close to the string knot, which must now be cut and carefully removed, then roll the distaff in the fan as in *Diagram 46*. Take care to keep the top ridge of the distaff and the apex of the fan together as you roll; if you are using a 'lantern', keep it on its spindle and keep the apex of the fan in contact with the part of the spindle which projects above the 'lantern'.

Pat the join gently down with the palm of the hand, set the distaff in its holder and tie the centre of the ribbon round what was the top of the fan with a fairly tight single knot, cross the two ends three or four times, according to the height of the distaff and tie a double bow (*Diagram 47*). Tuck up any ends which have become untidy, open out the short ends which were above the string knot to make an attractive plume at the top of the distaff and your flax is ready for spinning.

10. SPINNING ON THE WHEEL FROM THE DISTAFF. Arrange the distaff to the left and slightly in front of the orifice; if you use water or a wet sponge for damping your hand, have this also near the orifice and sit before the wheel in the usual position.

With a damp finger and thumb, draw down a few fibres from the bottom of the distaff with the left hand and twist them on to the yarn from the orifice. Treadle very slowly and, at first, keep the tension of the band loose, so that you will not feel hurried in any way. Continue drawing down fibres with the left hand, using the right hand while re-damping the left (*Diagram 47*).

If the dressing of the distaff has been well done, the fibres will draw down easily and continuously and the thickness of yarn can be comfortably controlled. If they begin to thin out too much, twist them by rolling the thumb along the forefinger and more will catch in, especially if the hand is moved up a little nearer to the distaff at the same time.

The left-hand movements are as follows:

Wet thumb on lower lip or in bowl; hold hand a few inches below bottom of distaff, draw out fibres with thumb and forefinger with slight twisting movement (thumb moving towards tip of finger); allow the hand to be drawn to within an inch of orifice with thumb closed on finger; release pressure of thumb slightly, rolling the yarn between it and the finger as the hand moves towards the distaff to draw more fibres (or to continue drawing the same fibres); this smooths the yarn.

It is not necessary to wet the hand for each draw; when required, the right hand can take over momentarily, so that spinning is not interrupted.

The distaff must be moved round a little at regular intervals, although a lantern head can be persuaded to turn of itself by moving the left hand up, to gather new fibres, always a little to the left of those already drawing down.

As with all spinning, movements should be as rhythmical as possible and the yarn should be moved along the guide hooks each time the distaff is turned.

As confidence is gained, the tension screw can be tightened very gradually so that yarn will not be too tightly twisted.

The perfect linen yarn is very smooth, only sufficiently twisted to give required strength, and very even. The beginner should strive for these qualities in that order. The fineness of a linen yarn to be spun must depend on the purpose for which it will be used as well as on the quality of the flax; generally speaking, it is permissible to use fine fibres for thick yarns but undesirable to use coarse fibres for thin yarns.

Long fibres, i.e. Line, should be used for warp; Tow can be spun into quite good weft.

## II. SOME DIFFICULTIES AND THEIR CAUSES.

(a) *Fibres refusing to draw down* or drawing down much too freely. This betokens a badly dressed distaff, insufficient care having been taken to ensure that NO fibres lay in straight lines as they were drawn from the strick to the lap. Layers of flax may also have been too thick.

Alas, the only remedy is a very wasteful one! Take the flax off the distaff, shake it thoroughly, hackle it thoroughly – a process which will give you plenty of tow – remove all loose straggling ends, both top and bottom, and begin again.

(b) *After spinning for some time, flax drops very low from the distaff.* This is also the result of insufficient care in spreading the fibres, but it can usually be remedied by tucking the flax under at this point and starting to draw from some other position.

(c) *The yarn is very hairy.* This may not always be entirely the fault of the spinner, though usually it is! Even with poor flax a smooth yarn can be produced with practice.

Always draw the fibres *down*, never draw against the pull from the wheel (i.e. endeavouring to retain the yarn); always smooth the yarn at the moment when the twist is running in, never let the finger and thumb get dry. Always smooth in the same direction, namely, towards the distaff and away from the orifice.

(d) *Knops, bits of boon, etc., sticking to the fibres* as they are drawn down. In perfectly dressed flax this is hardly ever found. The right hand should be used to remove them as they appear.

(e) *Yarn very tightly twisted*. This is the fault of the inexperienced spinner. Only practice will make it possible to draw the fibres steadily yet quickly enough to give a softly spun yarn. Never, NEVER hurry consciously; let speed come with experience.

From all the above paragraphs, you will have realized that good spinning depends almost entirely on the care with which the flax has been prepared and the distaff dressed. Even if you have had no part in the former operations, you have complete control over the latter and no pains must be spared to make it as perfect as possible. From a well-dressed distaff, every bit of flax can be used. As it reduces in size, the ribbon should be suitably re-tied, and if care is taken to spin from it equally all round, the very last fibres will draw down as conveniently as the first.

12. SPINNING THE TOW. Any waste short fibres should be hackled, first with the metal dog comb, and then with a strong fine hair comb. When they are freed from knots and tangles, prepare a roving about as thick as the little finger by drawing the fibres out to length and twisting a little in a clockwise direction.

The roving can be rolled into a ball and held in the lap while spinning or if you happen to possess a wheel fitted with a tow fork (*Diagram 48*), lace the roving round the prongs as shown and detach a length as needed.

Spin in the same way as for a worsted yarn, i.e. drawing out the fibres with the right hand and smoothing them back towards the roving as they twist. Of course the finger and thumb must be kept damp.

Yarn spun from tow with comparatively little twist can safely be used for weft.

## Chapter Nine

## SPINNING OTHER FIBRES

### A. SILK

1. The most perfect silk yarns are not spun at all in the ordinary meaning of the word. As every schoolboy knows, the caterpillar of the silk-worm moth spins a cocoon in which to shelter while it changes into a chrysalis. There are many varieties of silk *worm*, as the caterpillar is called, *Bombyx Mori* being the species most commonly bred in Europe.

When it is ready to spin, it attaches itself to any convenient twig or piece of straw by very fine filaments of silk which are really the beginnings of the cocoon. It makes the cocoon by squirting two streams of viscous liquid from glands near its mouth while moving its head from side to side in a kind of 'figure of eight' motion. The fluid and the gummy substance which accompanies it solidify in contact with the air and by the time the cocoon is completed, it consists of about 4,000 yards of continuous solidified filament firmly gummed together and is about the size of a peanut.

In order to reel off this filament, the chrysalis must be killed, before it breaks its way out, by subjecting the cocoon to considerable heat – this can be done in a domestic oven, if one can bear the resulting odour; the later stages of reeling are not for the amateur! When the chrysalids are dead, the cocoons are put into boiling water to soften the gum and, from above the vessel containing them, a revolving brush descends upon them; the loosened ends of the filaments adhere to the bristles and when the brush is raised the cocoons begin to unwind. One filament alone is much too fine for practical uses so, at this stage, from three to eight cocoons are separated from the rest and, after a little more preliminary unwinding, these are reeled in such a way as to make the result – to all intents and purposes – one single yarn. This is reeled silk, and two or more strands are twisted together, by the process known as THROW-

ING, to make yarns suitable for weaving and knitting. The amount of twist depends on the purpose for which it will be used; warp silk, known as ORGANZINE, has more than weft silk, or TRAM, which has scarcely any. It should be clearly understood that thrown, or NETT, silk is the choicest yarn.

2. SILK FOR SPINNING. At three stages of silk production, there is a fair amount of filament which, for one reason or another, cannot be reeled; this is the raw material of spun silk.

(a) *Floss.* This is the very fine silk by which the worm attaches itself to the straw preparatory to spinning the cocoon. It is extremely soft and weak and is often mixed with other waste silk.

(b) *Frisson* or *Strusa.* This is the waste from the first unwinding of the filament, preparatory to reeling; it is strong and very gummy.

(c) *Bassinet.* This consists of the last few layers of cocoons – the inside – when the supply is near exhaustion, and therefore less strong; silk from damaged cocoons; and silk, usually stained, from cocoons in which the chrysalis has died.

3. FRISSON – PREPARATION FOR SPINNING. This is quite the best form of silk for the handspinner. As obtained from the filature, nothing could possibly look more unprepossessing, resembling, as it does, untidy white straw. To prepare it, simmer it for $1\frac{1}{2}$ hours at a temperature of 195° F. (90° C.) in a solution made up in the proportion of 1 oz. of olive oil soap to 5 pints of water. (Lux can be used in the same proportion.) Rinse it in hot water and repeat with a fresh solution containing slightly less soap. This is the process known as DE-GUMMING. The soap solution dissolves the gum with which the filaments are coated and the process may have to be repeated a third time. If you intend to dye your spun silk, save the first 'boil-off' for use in the dye-bath. Rinse the silk thoroughly, hang it to dry and you will find it transformed into a soft, lustrous bundle of silk filaments about 2 yards long.

Fibres of such length cannot be spun direct, and the best way to deal with frisson is to wind the whole length round the prongs of a tow fork (*Diagram 48a*) or on a paper spool and cut lengths of $3\frac{1}{2}$–4 in. as required. Comb them on a carder as described for locks of fine wool for worsted spinning (*Chapter Five, par. 20*). A carder, a comb or a dog rake can be clamped on or near the spinning wheel and lengths of silk cut and prepared as required. Any waste left on the card can be used for mixture yarns (*Chapter Ten*).

4. SPINNING. The hands should be used in the same way as for worsted spinning except that the pressure of the thumb on the forefinger of the hand holding the fibres should be a little lighter than when handling wool and the draw will be rather shorter. When spinning on the wheel, increase the amount of twist and decrease the speed of wind-on (*Chapter Six, par. 3*) while you are getting used to the 'handle' of the silk. This will undoubtedly give a much over-spun yarn and, as confidence grows, the tension of the band can be increased and later the larger spindle whorl can be used.

From this type of silk waste, a lustrous, soft and even yarn of almost any size can be spun.

5. BASSINET – PREPARATION AND SPINNING. This is usually already de-gummed and to a certain extent freed from foreign matter; nevertheless, though very soft and fine, it contains many knops and tangles and is creamy fawn in colour.

It can be combed in small handfuls on a carder or wire brush and spun as described for frisson, or it can be carded, made into a rolag and drawn out almost as freely as wool. In neither case is it possible to spin a perfectly smooth or even yarn and the sensible thing to do is to make the best of its peculiar qualities by creating soft, knoppy yarns combining roughness of texture with the characteristic silky softness.

Frisson and Bassinet are obtainable from Lullingstone Silk Farm, Kent.

6. SILK SLIVERS. If frisson or bassinet is not obtainable from a silk farm, one can use silk slivers which are prepared by machine from silk wastes for use in power spinning (on cotton-spinning machines), but it is neither so easy to handle nor is it, as a rule, so good in quality.

### B. ANGORA RABBIT

1. HARVESTING THE FIBRE. These beautiful rabbits may be white, cream, fawn, smoky grey, black, or variegated in colour, but the fact that the fur accepts dyestuff in much the same way as wool makes white

the most popular. The length of staple varies from $\frac{1}{2}$ in. in very young rabbits to 7 or 8 in.; 3 to 5 in. is a fair average.

The fur is either clipped or plucked about every three months and for handspinning, plucked fur is undoubtedly the best. The best quality is obtained between the ages of 5 to 18 months; earlier yields are extremely fine and soft but may be too fine and too short for use alone (they may be carded with wool or silk for mixture yarns). After 18 months, the fur becomes steadily more and more hair-like and, though quite suitable for spinning, is no longer of first quality.

For the production of really good yarns, the equivalent of careful sorting is just as essential as for wool. The fur differs in character in various parts of the animal as well as with its age. The longest staple is found on the back and shoulders, with a tendency to coarse hairs towards the tail. Fur from the under parts is shorter and softer with a slight crimp and is somewhat tender. On the upper parts there are always some long hairs which should be pulled out before plucking; they spoil both yarn and fabric made from it because they are resistant to dyestuffs and they shed easily.

Because the various sorts of fur handle so differently, they should be kept separate. The fur is very light and delicate and the most convenient way of preparing it for the spinner is to lay it out flat, as soon as it is plucked, in a paper-lined tin, putting a layer of paper between each layer of fur, but not compressing it in any way; the tin should be airtight.

2. SPINNING. Angora which is to be spun by itself should on no account be carded; if plucked with discrimination and packed as described, it should be in perfect condition for handspinning.

Its smooth softness is displayed to perfection when spun to a reasonably fine yarn using the hands in the same way as when spinning combed wool for worsted. It is quite possible to work on a spindle so long as the whorl is light in weight; a heavy spindle makes the production of a fine yarn impossible, not because it cannot be made strong, but because the fibres slip past one another so very easily. If your spindle is very heavy, try spinning it in a bowl or saucer so that the yarn does not bear its full weight (par. H.3, page 100).

When spinning on the wheel, hold the fibres as in Diagram 31, using the stronger, coarser fur for practice. Reduce the speed of wind and increase the twist (*Chapter Six, par. 3*) until you grow accustomed to the fibre.

3. SOME DIFFICULTIES. *Joining on to the starting yarn.* Use a hand-spun woollen starting yarn and twist the first fibres of angora on to it with a wet thumb. If the yarn breaks while spinning, the end must be untwisted before one can join on new fibres.

*Judging the amount of twist required.* This is very difficult with all short fibres, especially very smooth ones. Practise making, at first, a very hard-twisted yarn, gradually increasing the speed of wind in relation to the amount of twist until the yarn no longer holds at all, then decreasing it by slow degrees until you have a yarn which is strong, yet soft. Remember that the yarn will soften when washed.

*Spinning the very short fibres.* The hand movements are exactly as already described, but must be performed very quickly in relation to the rate of treadling because the length drawn out at a time is so small. Very short fibres – less than an inch – and fur which is at all matted should be carded with good quality Down wool (*page 110, par. 3b*).

N.B. From the very· fine and tender fibres, the more experienced spinner will be able to spin fine yarns for plying (*Chapter Ten, par. A*).

### C. ANGORA

This, rather confusingly, is the name of a goat which is native to the uplands of Asia Minor but which is bred in great numbers both in South Africa and in the state of Texas. It yields wool known as MOHAIR (from the Arabic *mukhayyar* = a coarse hair cloth) which is very white, long stapled and lustrous. Because of its structure, fabrics made from it do not crease. Fine, strong, very lustrous yarn can be spun by the worsted method, especially from the hair of young animals, but one's only chance of doing so in this country is through the good offices of the curator of a zoo.

### D. CAMEL HAIR AND WOOL

1. Like many other animals which have to endure cold, the Bactrian camel bears long coarse hair and, beneath it, fine very soft wool. It is a

native of the districts of climatic extremes of Central Asia, and because of its structure, the wool and hair have extraordinarily good insulating qualities.

With the coming of warm weather, the coat begins to 'rise' and it falls off in great matted lumps of wool and hair mixed; at the time of the moult, it is the job of one member of each caravan to follow in its wake to gather them up.

For commercial use, the fibres are combed; the tops being the coarse *hairs*; the noils, in this instance, are the masses of valuable soft *wool*. Though it can be dyed, it cannot be bleached to take light clear colours; but the natural fawns and tans are sufficiently lovely in themselves for this to be no disadvantage.

2. PREPARATION FOR SPINNING. Remove as many of the long coarse hairs as possible by pulling them away from the wool; this is not as difficult as it sounds because they are so long and so very coarse. In sufficient quantity, they would spin a good rug yarn. Take a handful of the remaining wool; if it is matted, tear it apart as gently as possible and then tease it lightly to remove any foreign matter. This may be very difficult because seeds, straws and so forth adhere to the very soft wool with great persistence. Tease by pulling the hands – and the wool – very quickly apart so that the wool floats in mid-air and the heavier matter falls to the ground.

Card it as you would card wool, but instead of rolling it into a rolag, follow the action shown in *Diagram 23* by rolling it up by hand across the width of the card as in *Diagram 49*.

During the stages of carding, as many as possible of the remaining long hairs should be pulled away.

3. SPINNING. Camel wool has little felting quality and there is no particular advantage to be gained by spinning it woollen fashion, especially for a warp yarn. By rolling the fibres up as described above, they are laid more or less parallel but with enough variation in direction to provide a certain amount of air space. Once one is accustomed to the extreme fineness and softness, it is possible to draw out a fair length by waiting for the twist to accumulate as when making woollen yarn (*Chapter Six, par. 5*), but the fibres should be allowed to come from the

fingers and thumb of the drawing hand somewhat fanwise, as in worsted spinning.

The very finest, softest wool can be carded, made into a rolag and spun, woollen fashion, for weft.

Exquisite yarns in the beautiful natural colours can be spun; the fineness of the fibres invites fine spinning, but thick soft yarns are equally satisfactory. It can be carded with suitably chosen wool to give harder wearing qualities. Camel hair, if not too coarse, can be combed and spun worsted fashion to make warm, light rugs. Both wool and hair may need a little oil.

### E. DOG COMBINGS, ETC.

Many dogs yield combings or clippings which can be spun into useful yarns by whichever method is best suited to the length and character of the fibres. Poodle clippings, for example, make a very pleasant 'woollen' yarn while the lustre of Spaniel hair needs a worsted spin. The addition of a little oil prior to combing or carding may make spinning easier.

Combings or clippings should be stored until wanted in an air-tight container in a cool place, preferably with a moth deterrent such as paradichlorbenzine.

No instance of the use of cat's hair for spinning has ever come to light but it would be quite possible to spin combings of a fine haired Persian, especially carded with suitable wool. The author's experiments with a mixture of Siamese and camel are not to be recommended!

### F. OTHER ANIMAL HAIR

Many other hairs, wools and furs can be used for handspinning, llama, alpaca, vicuna and Kashmir goat, to name but a few; in this country, our only chance of experimenting with these and other animals not native to Britain is through the kindly help of the curator of a local zoological collection. Camel wool and hair can certainly be bought in small quantities in this way at the appropriate time of year.

### G. HEMP, JUTE AND RAMIE

These are all plant fibres obtained by processes similar to those used to produce flax; all of them can be spun much as flax is spun, though not necessarily from a distaff.

*Jute* is one of the lowest grades of natural fibres in use; it is harsh, not very strong in relation to its fibre thickness, and when used, as it often is, to adulterate better yarns, it betrays its presence in a very short time because it yellows when exposed to light. It is universally used for making sacks.

It can be spun by hand using a little oil instead of water, but it is not particularly rewarding.

*Hemp* is softer and stronger than jute. If the fibres are not too long, it can even be spun from a distaff. Very long fibres of any kind can sometimes be made reasonably tractable by hanging them, lightly bound, on a wall hook, drawing them down as if from a distaff. Hemp makes a good warp yarn for handwoven rugs.

*Ramie*, also called *China grass* or *Rhea*, is grown and processed in China but is now almost unobtainable in England. In many ways it is not unlike flax; indeed, material made from it in the East is sometimes known as Chinese linen. It lacks the peculiar strength of flax although it is softer and more lustrous.

*Sisal*, *Manilla hemp* and many other plant fibres can be spun into strong yarns, if not by hanging up, then by cutting the fibres into manageable lengths and working from the hand. Usually the plant fibres need wetting to spin them smoothly.

### H. COTTON

1. In this country, cotton is rarely obtainable, and then only in the form of slivers prepared, at every stage, for use on spinning machinery. It is not a native plant and there is no long tradition of handspinning here as there is in the East and on the African continent.

2. PREPARING THE FIBRES. The cotton fibres are the downy covering of the seeds of the cotton plant which are contained in a pod, usually called a BOLL (*Diagram 50*). When the bolls ripen and burst, they are picked by hand and the cotton is separated from the seed. If possible, cotton for handspinning should be obtained, if not on the boll, then at least on the seeds (*Diagram 50a*). At the time of writing this is virtually

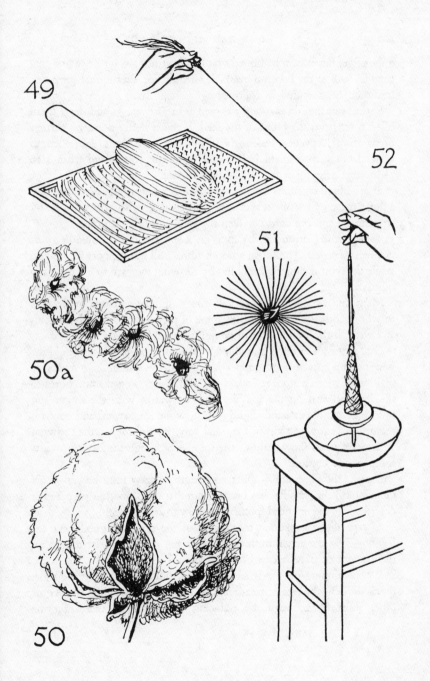

49

52

51

50a

50

impossible, but it is to be hoped that this may not always be so and that supplies will again become available, if only for educational purposes. It should be prepared as follows:

Spread out the fibres round the seed as in *Diagram 51* and draw them off – away from the point of the seed. If this is deftly done, no further preparation is needed unless the fibres are very short. Fibre length varies from ½ to 1 in. in Indian and American cotton and from 1 to 1½ in. in the Egyptian and Sea Island varieties.

Short-fibred cotton is easier to spin if it is whipped up, i.e. made into a fluffy mass, by beating it with a flexible twig, or with a 'bow' made by stretching a smooth cord between the two ends of a thin cane.

3. SPINNING. Cotton can be spun on a spindle, but the spindle must not be suspended. The short, smooth fibres will not support its weight, while the twist is running in, unless by allowing the yarn to be much too tightly twisted.

Many and varied are the ways of using a spindle practised by peoples to whom cotton is a native plant, some of them extraordinarily difficult and with all the appearances of conjuring tricks!

One of the easier ways of making a yarn with the spindle is to hold the whipped-up cotton in the upper hand, spin the spindle in a saucer or shallow bowl on a stool (*Diagram 52*), and having joined some fibres to the starting yarn on the spindle, draw upwards, with the finger and thumb of the upper hand slightly open, while the lower hand controls the upward moving twist in the usual way. By this means, the growing yarn never bears the weight of the spindle, although the latter provides some of the tension.

Because the fibres are so short, the length of draw must be very short indeed until the 'handle' has become familiar. With cotton prepared as described, an experienced spinner can draw to arm's length.

A very slight *untwisting* movement of the upper thumb along the forefinger, at the actual moment of drawing, makes it easier to control the amount of fibre released from above.

When spinning on the wheel, the chief difficulty is to suit the short quick draw to the rate of treadling and the speed of winding on. As for other short fibres, begin by reducing the latter and increasing the twist, readjusting both when you have learned to control the fibres.

Hold both hands near the orifice and draw out the fibres fanwise, using the slight untwisting movement of the left thumb along the forefinger to give added control.

Aim at producing a smooth, even, strong, but not over-twisted yarn. More twist is needed for warp than for weft, unless a plied yarn is to be used. The fine fibres lend themselves very naturally to the spinning of very fine yarn and, generally speaking, very coarse yarns are more happily achieved by plying (*Chapter Ten*) than as single yarns.

Cotton prepared for machine spinning can be used by handspinners in the form of slivers. It is not so easy to handle because of the rigorous treatment it has suffered; the fibres are shorter and it seems lifeless and mechanical compared with the cotton taken by hand from the seed. The methods of spinning are the same.

## I. SYNTHETIC FIBRES

All the man-made fibres can be spun by hand if so desired in the same way as cotton slivers are spun. Although they are all produced as continuous filaments, they are, more often than not, cut into short lengths and spun on cotton-spinning machinery. They are more difficult to handle because they are alien to the traditional methods of handspinning which, it must be remembered, came into being to serve the needs of the natural fibres. The synthetic yarns, on the other hand, owe their character almost entirely to the demand for cheap yarns which can be used on power looms to produce comparatively inexpensive fabrics as quickly as possible – time being another word for money.

Whether the handspinner will succeed, or will ever want to succeed, in reconciling the apparently irreconcilable, has yet to be seen. For those who have a liking for the handle of the various synthetic materials there is certainly plenty of scope for using them in new ways.

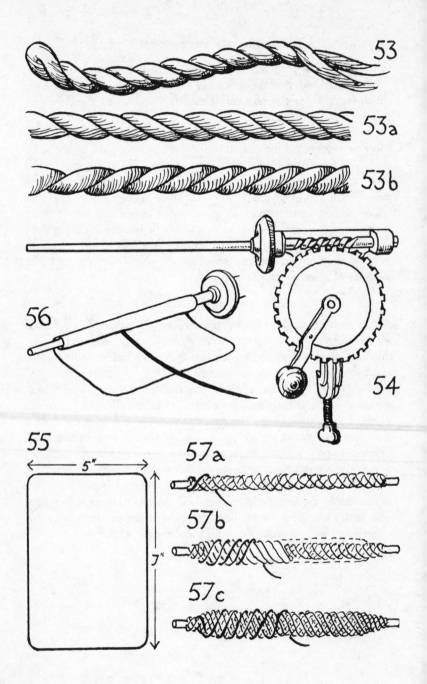

53

53a

53b

56

54

55

5"

7"

57a

57b

57c

*Chapter Ten*

# THE SPINNING WHEEL IN DESIGN

THE enthusiast who has taken time and trouble to learn how to handle spindle and wheel, and who has come to understand something of yarn construction, will find an added pleasure in experimenting with the making of somewhat more complicated yarns. As a preliminary to this fascinating subject, let us first discover what can be done about making plied yarns.

### A. FOLDED, DOUBLED OR PLIED YARNS (*Plié* = folded)

The reader with his early experiences still freshly in mind will have little difficulty in imagining how the first 2-ply yarn came into existence; the much over-spun yarn which folds back on itself and twists into a rope, before the harassed spinner has had time to straighten it out and wind it on the spindle, must have been as familiar in the kingdom of the Pharaohs as it is to us! If a tightly spun yarn is *folded* or *doubled* in half, the reason for the names variously given to these yarns will be readily understood; possibly lengths of yarn were actually so folded in early times to give greater strength. If you examine this folded piece of yarn, you will discover that the two yarns (or, in this case, the two ends of the one yarn) twist together in a direction opposite to the twist of the single yarn (*Diagram 53*), i.e. two tightly S-twisted SINGLES will ply naturally in a Z twist.

I. SPINNING A 2-PLY YARN ON A SPINDLE. The simplest 2 ply is made by spinning together two Z-twisted singles with an S twist. This can be done very easily on a spindle from two previously spun cones of yarn placed on a stand made from cardboard and knitting needles (*Diagram 14*).

Tie the two ends of yarn to a starting yarn of the correct twist (the reverse of that of the two yarns) and allow the yarns to pass one on each side of the middle finger of the left hand instead of controlling them with the finger and thumb as when spinning. Spin the spindle with the other hand and allow the yarns to slide between the fingers until the spindle almost touches the floor. Wait until sufficient twist has run into the yarns, then wind on as usual. In some ways, it is easier to ply yarns on the spindle than on the wheel but it is, of course, very much slower. Three, four or more SINGLES (the name given to any once-spun yarn) can be plied in the same way.

Z-twisted singles can, of course, be plied with a Z twist and S-twisted singles with an S twist. The resulting yarn is rather harder in character because the original twist is intensified. It is not a good method for worsted spun yarns as a rule; a lustrous yarn, which is worsted spun, has its fibres lying parallel to its twist, if two such yarns are plied together with the *reverse* twist, the fibres will lie roughly parallel to the length of the yarn, thus increasing the lustre (*Diagram 53a*). In yarns where the ply-twist is not reversed, the fibres lie across the width of the yarn (*Diagram 53b*).

2. PLYING ON THE WHEEL. Two or three spare bobbins are needed to save time in winding. If your wheel is an old one, it may be impossible to obtain bobbins which will fit it and, as well-plied yarns cannot be made from balls of yarn, you will need some kind of spool winder; *Diagram 54* shows a typical example. Cut rectangles of strong, but not stiff paper (*Diagram 55*), wrap them round the winder-spindle with an end of the yarn from the spinning wheel bobbin, as in *Diagram 56*, and wind on the yarn as in *Diagrams 57a, b* and *c*. Note very carefully how the layers of yarn are packed on.

If you are a weaver and possess a spool rack, your spools or bobbins can be arranged on the lower rails; if not, choose a box of wood or strong card, wide enough to take two bobbins side by side – leaving each room to run freely – and bore holes for two long knitting needles, size 14 (*Diagram 58*). Have this on the floor to your left.

Arrange the yarns to be plied as shown, allow them to pass – each one separately – between the fingers of the left hand, tie them to a starting yarn, help them through the orifice and over the first guide hook, then begin treadling fairly quickly and absolutely regularly.

Allow the yarns to pass through the fingers freely, detaining them no more than is needed to produce the desired amount of twist. If your yarns have been spun with the Z twist (wheel turning clockwise), the wheel should revolve anti-clockwise when plying.

This all sounds very simple, but some practice is needed to make a really good folded yarn. One yarn paying *out* more freely than the others, uneven treadling, unsteady rate of paying *in* the yarns, all may cause uneven work.

Wool, hair and cotton are the yarns most frequently plied; because of its great strength as a singles yarn, flax is very seldom treated in this way.

3. DESIGN IN PLIED YARNS. Even within the very narrow limits of design already described, there can be much variety. For example, the singles to be plied may be lightly spun and the plying done tightly, or *vice versa*; both singles and plying can be tightly spun, or both may be light in spinning. One of the best ways of making a very soft, yet strong wool yarn for knitting, or for a weaver's warp, is to spin two very fine singles yarns so lightly that they just hold and no more, and to ply these with as little spin as will make a safe yarn.

Bearing in mind the principles explained, one can produce very interesting 2-fold yarns by varying the characteristics of the two singles. Here are some experiments to try, at first in wool, later adapting them for cotton or silk:

(a) *Diagram 59*. Two lightly twisted, not too fine worsted spun yarns, one S twisted, the other Z twisted. Ply with S or Z twist.

(b) *Diagram 60*. A thick, soft, S-twisted woollen yarn and a thin worsted spun with a Z twist. Ply with a Z twist.

N.B. In both these the effect results from the fact that the process of plying *adds* twist to one of the two singles and *reduces* it in the other.

(c) *Diagram 61*. A thick, softly spun woollen or worsted singles and a fine, firmly spun worsted, both with the same twist. Ply with the reverse twist, paying in slowly enough to give a fair amount of spin.

(d) Two silk frisson yarns used as in (a) above (*Diagram 59*).

4. HEAVY PLIED YARNS. A number of plied yarns can be plied

together again to give heavy cord-like effects. It should be realized that such a cord would be quite different in appearance and handle from the 'cable' yarn which would result from plying together the same number of singles. For example, three 3-ply yarns, plied together, will give a firm cordy yarn; if the nine singles used to make it were spun into a 9-ply yarn, the result would be a softer cable. In both, firmness would be increased if the twist were always in the same direction.

Very interesting cord yarns may be made by using one of the fancy yarns described in *Section* C below as one of the yarns to be plied.

N.B. When drying after finishing, plied yarns should be stretched (*Chapter Eleven, par. 1d, Diagram 78*).

### B. MIXTURE YARNS

One of the simplest, and perhaps the most annoying, forms of mixture yarn is one in which the different matchings from a fleece must all be carded together because there is not enough of any particular one to complete the piece of work on hand. Although one should resort to this practice only in an emergency, it is wiser to do this than to use the different matchings in various parts of the same cloth or knitting. However, this example shall serve as an illustration of the mixing of fibres on the cards.

1. MIXING WOOL ON THE CARDS. Tease the wools to be mixed in the usual way, put each variety to be used in a separate box and have these boxes arranged around you. Spread a very thin film of wool from each in turn right across the card; do *not* put a tuft of one here and a tuft of another there. Card and make the rolag as usual and spin in the usual way. Make quite sure that you take the same quantity from any one box each time you card.

2. MAKING COLOUR MIXTURES. This is a very delightful occupation.

(a) *A variable coloured fleece.* Let us assume that we are dealing with a fleece in which the good wool is partly white, partly brown-black and partly grey – a not uncommon occurrence in a Welsh fleece. Some of each colour might be kept apart to be spun separately, a fourth colour could be made by mixing some of the brown-black with the grey, and a background colour for the whole colour scheme could be created by

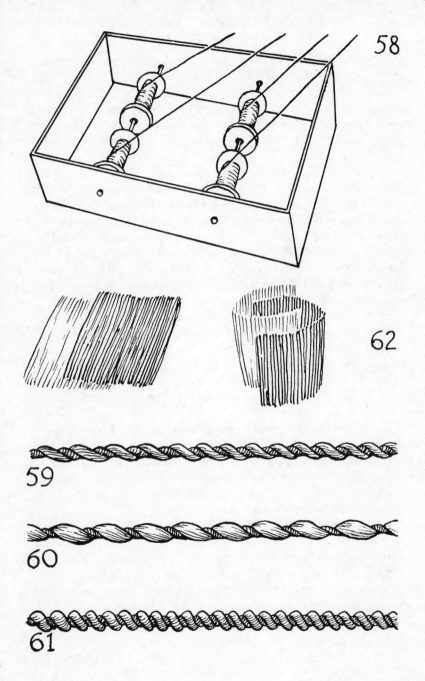

58

62

59

60

61

mixing the white, the grey and the brown-black on the cards as described above to obtain a lovely broken fawn-grey.

(b) *Using dyed fleece* (see 'Your Yarn Dyeing'). From fleece dyed a good yellow (weld), a rich red (cochineal) and a clear blue (indigo) used with a scoured but undyed white, it is no exaggeration to say that thousands of different colours can be blended by varying the proportions of the four lots of fleece. Why not try?

Use considerably more olive oil when teasing scoured and dyed fleece to replace the natural grease which has been removed.

(c) *'Heather Mixtures'*, or any other mixture of harmonizing colours. In this kind of colour mixture each colour in the yarn should be distinguishable from the others, so in this case, having teased the wool in separate lots – assuming there are three colours – spread a sixth of the surface of the card with each colour in turn and card and spin as usual. If you prefer a very indefinite colour scheme, spread the colours on the card in the sequence a, b, c, a, b, c, a, b, c, etc.

(d) *Knap yarns.* Small knaps of contrasting colour can be put into a woollen yarn in one of two ways. Card the basic coloured wool in the usual way, but before taking the wool off card L to make the rolag, i.e. immediately after the stage shown in *Diagram 22*, sprinkle the surface of the wool with very small, short stapled bits of strongly contrasting coloured fleece. Pat them down with the back of card R and take off the rolag as usual.

By the other method, they are put in while spinning. Keep a shallow box or tray filled with the 'knaps' near whichever hand you are using to control the twist and insert one at regular intervals. These make more definite spots than when added to the carded wool but tend to come out more easily in wear. Bad cuts in shearing (fribby wool) or noils from worsted spinning can be dyed for use as 'knaps'.

(e) *Coloured ply yarns.* A very simple and effective yarn can be made by plying two different coloured singles; by combining colour changes with some of the suggestions given in the section on plied yarns one can make extremely attractive yarns.

3. FIBRE MIXTURES. In the world of commercial yarns, nowadays, to one pure unmixed yarn there must be thousands in which, for

economic reasons, two or more substances are used. As a rule, the only reasons which justify mixing fibres in hand-spun yarns are to give strength to otherwise delicate fibres, to provide a basis of long fibres for those which are too short to spin and to enhance the appearance of both fibres used, generally by contrast.

The ancient rule of 'animal with animal and vegetable with vegetable' is very sound in many respects, if only because methods of dyeing the one are often extremely damaging to the other. This applies to both traditional and modern dyestuffs. In this simple classification, silk is, of course, reckoned as animal and the various rayons are broadly speaking vegetable in origin. Nylon has, on the whole, greater affinity with the animal fibres through its approximation to protein.

Owing to its very individual characteristics, flax does not lend itself happily to mixtures.

3a. MIXTURE BY PLYING. The most obvious way of mixing two fibres in one yarn would seem to be to ply single yarns of each. Very interesting yarns can be made in this way although certain difficulties may arise if they are to be used in a weaver's warp. If you have succeeded in spinning a number of different fibres, you will have noticed, no doubt, that the resulting yarns vary considerably in their ability to extend when stretched and to regain their original length when the strain is relaxed. A well-spun woollen yarn from a good Down wool is almost like a piece of elastic: a worsted yarn spun from the same wool would be less so. Wool has this quality of resilience to a greater degree than any other fibre, but it varies considerably among different breeds of fleece. In the Long, Lustre wools it exists to a lesser extent than in Down wools and some of the very coarse, hairy Mountain wools seem to lack it almost entirely. Of the other fibres, flax is almost without 'give', a fact all too familiar to weavers; hair and fur is always elastic to a greater or lesser degree, depending on the presence or absence of waviness in the fibres. Nett silk is very elastic, spun silk rather less so; cotton has more elasticity than linen.

These characteristics must be borne closely in mind when designing yarns in which one fibre is plied with another if they are likely to be subjected to much strain. If one singles yarn is very elastic and the other is not, the inelastic yarn will bear the brunt of this strain and must therefore be strong enough to do so. For example, a silk singles, plied with a wool singles, might be quite satisfactory because even if the silk were less elastic than the wool, it would be likely to be strong; if baby angora yarn were used instead of the silk, the angora might well break as soon as the yarn were stretched, for not only is baby angora yarn less elastic than wool, it is also less strong.

3b. MIXING BEFORE SPINNING.

(a) *Angora, camel or other fine short fibres with wool.* It goes without saying that only the finer wools should be used for this purpose; to card these fine fibres with a coarse fleece is to sacrifice the qualities of both fibres. The proportion of fine fibre to wool must remain a matter of individual choice but quite a little wool makes it possible to spin the very shortest fibres.

Lay the wool on the card first, then spread on the other fibre, as evenly distributed as possible, card in the usual way and for a woollen spun yarn make a rolag.

If the mixture is to be worsted spun, remove the fibre from the card as explained in *Chapter Nine, Section D, par. 2, Diagram 49*, and spin from one end of the roll. If the wool is very 'nappy' (i.e. with very short fine fibres and tiny lumps which roll into little balls on the card), comb it before beginning to card the mixture.

(b) *Silk waste with wool.* If the silk fibres are not too short, an effective yarn can be made by spreading the card with a little wool and a little silk in turn until the full width is covered by alternate strips of silk and wool fibre. Card and make either a rolag or a roll of lengthwise fibres (*Diagram 49*) according to the kind of yarn to be made.

For a more thorough mixture, lay the wool on the card first, then the silk; card, as when colour mixing, very thoroughly and make a rolag for woollen yarn or a crosswise roll for worsted spinning. This is also the most suitable method when the silk fibres are very short.

(c) *Dog clippings or combings with wool.* It is difficult to give any definite guidance as to the type of wool to use because the character of the fibres varies so much. If the yarn is to be used for personal wear, let the wool be finer than the dog hair. If carpet wool is to be spun, the wool can be of the coarse, long, hard-wearing type such as the Blackface. Poodle wool, especially from a young animal, could well be used with a Down type wool, but the lustrous longer wools are more akin to most other dog hairs.

Mix on the carders if possible; if not practicable because of the length of fibre, comb a small handful of each, spread each combed handful out a little and fold one with the other as in *Diagram 62*. When spun worsted fashion, the two fibres will draw out together without much difficulty.

### C. FANCY YARNS

Having developed machines which would produce the perfect regularity in yarn to which handspinners of the past aspired, yarn manufacturers have, in recent years, worked to reproduce by machine the unevenly spun yarns which were deliberately used by handweavers earlier in the present century, in their revolt against the lifeless precision of machine work. If the reader will refer to *Diagrams 63* to *75*, he will, no doubt, recognize the origins of the *Slub* in his own badly drafted efforts when learning, with its thick unspun lumps and thin overtwisted lengths; *Spiral* yarns he will certainly make when learning to ply and *Snarls* he will know only too well, since overspinning is the besetting sin of the beginner.

These and many other things may be done with justification if they are done with intention and for some particular effect, whether for knitting or weaving.

1. UNEVENLY PLIED YARNS. These are effective in two colours or two strongly contrasting fibres. Spin a singles of each colour and when plying with the opposite twist, alternately retard them and hurry them in to obtain the effect shown in *Diagram 63*.

2. SLUB YARNS. Card or comb the fibre as usual and use the hands as for worsted spinning; draw out short lengths in the usual way, and at regular intervals draw a thick lump by putting the finger and thumb on the wide end of the fan of fibres when drawing them out instead of on the apex of the triangle.

N.B. Take care not to make the 'slub' too thick to pass through the orifice and over the guide hooks.

*Diagram 64* shows a singles slub.

*Diagram 65* shows a 2-ply slub in two versions, *a and b:*

(a) Spin two single slubs of a different colour and with very light twist. Ply in the reverse twist with the slubs coinciding.

(b) Spin similar singles, ply with reverse twist with the slubs co-inciding with the thin sections.

Very accurate spinning is needed, and for this and most of the other fancy yarns, the two singles for plying should be arranged so that one runs in the left hand and the other in the right so that each can be controlled independently.

*Diagram 66* shows a fancy slub. Spin a Z-twisted single slub yarn in wool and a fine S-twisted worsted or silk singles. Ply them with a Z twist, controlling one in each hand, allowing the thin yarn to wind round the thin parts of the slub, but plying it normally over the thick parts. As the right hand is usually more deft, control the thin yarn with it, and hold the slub steadily in the left.

A very similar effect can be obtained by spinning a thick, soft, woollen yarn with a very light twist and winding the finer yarn round this between intervals of normal plying. It is more difficult to obtain a regular interval than when one has the slub as a guide.

## 3. THE CORKSCREW OR SPIRAL

*Diagram 67.* Spin two lightly twisted yarns. Ply them with reverse twist, controlling one in each hand; retard one slightly and allow the other to run very freely. The free running yarn will twist round the other.

*Diagram 68* shows a more clearly defined version. Spin a full, soft, yarn and, with the reverse twist, spin a thin firm silk, cotton or worsted yarn. Ply in the same direction as the twist of the thin yarn, retarding this and allowing the soft yarn to pass freely.

## 4. BEAD YARNS.

*Diagram 69.* These yarns are made from a thick and a fine singles plied in the normal way and with the reverse twist.

## 5. SNARL AND BOUCLÉ.

*Diagram 70.* Spin a very much twisted fine yarn and a rather thicker yarn with average amount of twist. Ply them with the reverse twist, very slightly retarding the normally spun yarn and paying in the over-

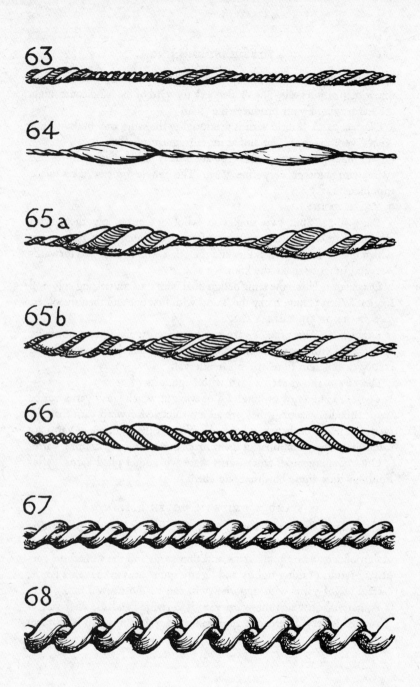

63

64

65 a

65 b

66

67

68

spun yarn, first, normally, then – very suddenly – freely and repeating this at regular intervals. The sudden jerk forward of the hand controlling the hard-twisted yarn produces the 'snarl'.

*Diagram 71*. A Bouclé yarn is produced in the same way but with the 'snarls' very much smaller and at more frequent intervals.

(Machine-spun yarns of this type are usually again plied, with reverse twist with another very fine yarn. The whole process takes place simultaneously.)

6. KNOT YARNS.

*Diagram 72*. Spin two singles in wool or cotton, ply them with reverse twist, alternating passages of normal plying with passages in which one of the yarns winds round the other – backwards and forwards – several times to make the knot.

*Diagram 73*. This is the same design used with two contrasting coloured singles. When plying, make the 'knot' with first one and then the other.

7. NEP, KNOP OR TUFT YARNS.

*Diagram 74*. This type of yarn can be made by plying two normally spun yarns with reverse twist while inserting small tufts of contrasting colour or different fibre at regular intervals.

*Diagram 75* shows such a yarn with large tufts.

These are but a few of hundreds of ways in which fancy yarns can be spun. Broadly speaking, they are all less suitable for warp yarn than for weft, but many of them can be used as warp if the component yarns are carefully chosen; a number of them make most attractive knitting yarns.

One requirement all fancy yarns share with other plied yarns – after finishing they must be dried stretched.

### D. S AND Z TWIST IN WOVEN DESIGN

Even without the use of fancy yarns, the weaver lays the foundation of his cloth design on the spinning wheel. Apart from the variety of design obtainable by using thick and thin yarns and the sometimes surprising results of using tightly and lightly spun yarns in the same fabric, careful use of yarns with opposite twist can be most rewarding.

A material of which the warp yarn is Z-twisted and the weft yarn is S-twisted is very different in appearance from one in which both yarns

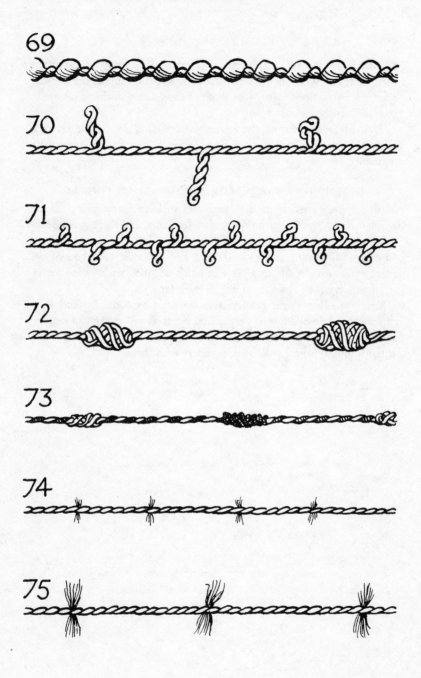

69

70

71

72

73

74

75

are the same; indeed, a material in which a warp stripe of Z-twisted yarn alternates with one of S-twisted yarn will have almost the appearance of a two-colour stripe – the result of the shading of the fibres in the two differently twisted yarns.

This paragraph forms the barest introduction to this interesting subject in which the spinner can find plenty of scope for the exercise of ingenuity.

### E. DESIGNING YARNS FROM MACHINE-SPUN SINGLES

Many of the experiments in plying and making fancy yarns can be adapted for use with machine-spun singles yarns, and there is considerable enjoyment to be found in conjuring from a dull, mechanical looking yarn some interesting and unusual effect. For a weaver, too, the unity of effect which may result, in a piece of work designed with varied yarns, all of which have grown from one, is most satisfying.

Fancy woollen yarns, particularly, are hard to come by and very expensive, while odd lots of very uninteresting woollen yarns of reasonable quality can usually be bought fairly cheaply; a few enjoyable hours at the spinning wheel will work wonders with them.

*Chapter Eleven*

# PREPARING SPUN YARNS FOR USE

AFTER spinning, most yarns require some kind of treatment to make them suitable for weaving and knitting, wool and other animal fibres must be freed from grease, linen must be softened and possibly bleached, and although silk can be used straight from the spinning wheel, it is the better for a little after-treatment.

1. WOOL. If the yarn is to remain undyed, some weavers prefer to use it 'in the grease', i.e. unscoured, and scour the cloth in the piece. Knitters, as a rule, find it more satisfactory to scour the yarn first because of the difficulty of making allowance for the exact amount of shrinkage. This can be overcome by knitting a sample piece and measuring both dimensions before and after scouring. Where a compact surface effect is required, this is well worth the trouble.

(a) *Steeping*. Make sure that all skeins are tied as described in *Chapter Four, par. 12*, and shown in *Diagrams 17a, b* and *c*, then lay them in clear, hot (50–55° C.) water and allow them to steep until the water is cold. N.B. Soft water or rain water must be used for all scouring processes if possible; if the water is hard, it may be softened, to some extent, by using ammonia or a water softener such as Calgon, according to the directions given with the product.

Preliminary steeping is necessary to reduce the risk of felting the yarn. Use enough water to well cover the yarn.

(b) *Soap Scouring*. Make a full lather with a good olive oil soap or Lux in enough water to well cover the yarn and, when it cools sufficiently to put the hand in (45–50° C.), immerse the wool; it should float freely and be in no way compressed. Loosen the yarn gently where the ties come, taking very great care not to break the yarn. Turn the skeins over once or twice but on no account 'wash' them. Keep clearly in mind the fact that the best and quickest way to make wool *felt up* is by rubbing and squeezing it in hot soapy water! Let this thought deter you from handling it more than is absolutely necessary. Leave the yarn in the suds overnight if possible, then rinse it once in warm water, still handling it lightly. Make a second lot of suds using rather less soap or Lux and wait until it is cooler than before (35–40° C.) before putting in the yarn. Again leave it in for some hours, then rinse thoroughly in tepid water. (If the yarn is still slightly greasy, soak it in suds once again, entering it at the lower temperature.)

When scouring a large quantity, it is easier to handle the skeins if a thick, very smooth string or a length of white tape is passed through them and tied to the handles of the washing bath or bucket (*Diagram 76*).

N.B. When lifting wet skeins, always hold them by the free tie (*Diagram 17c*), NEVER pick them up by the skein tie (*Diagram 17b*).

Several soakings in a soap bath leave the wool in much better condition than one or two baths in which it is squeezed and constantly turned. When dealing with a large quantity, it does no harm to use a suction washing 'dolly' (*Diagram 77*) when the suds are nearly cold.

(c) *Scouring with a chemical detergent – Lissapol C.* This is an Imperial Chemical Industries product. It has certain advantages over soap scouring, especially in hard water. The temperature of the water can be higher and the wool can be squeezed more freely without undue risk of felting. Use one tablespoonful to a gallon of water: two soakings, each beginning at about 55° C., are usually sufficient.

(d) *Drying.* When the skeins are sufficiently scoured, rinse them until the water is clear and squeeze but do not wring them. It is quite safe to put them through a mangle if the roller pressure is adjusted for light wringing.

Woollen spun yarn can be dried without tension. Skeins should hang on a rod rather than by their ties. If possible dry wool in a good draught.

Worsted spun yarn and plied yarns should be stretched until dry. The niddy-noddy is quite satisfactory for one skein, so is a floor swift. If many skeins are to be dried, hang them on a rod suspended in three or four places, slip another rod through the bottom of the skeins and either weight it or tie it so that the skeins are tensioned (*Diagram 78*).

2. ANGORA RABBIT. Angora fur has little if any natural grease and

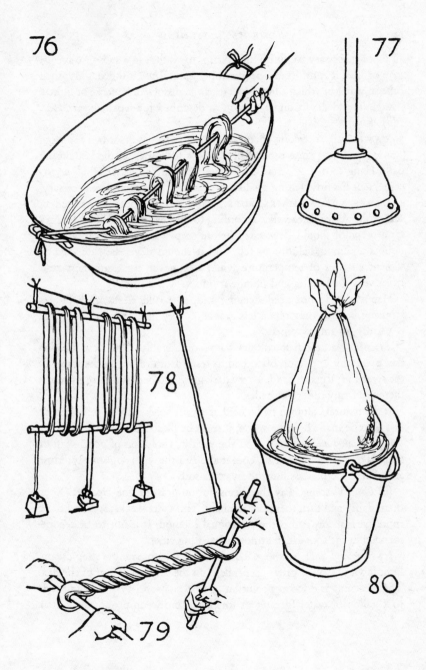

76

77

78

79

80

all that is necessary to 'finish' the yarn is to wash it in a suds of olive oil soap or Lux at comfortable hand temperature. Rinse it thoroughly, then rinse in water in which a little soap has been dissolved. Squeeze or lightly mangle it and dry it under tension as described for worsted yarn (*par. 1 (d) above*).

3. CAMEL WOOL. Scour once, or at most twice, as described for wool (*par. 1 (b) above*); rinse thoroughly using a little soap in the last rinsing bath. Hang to dry as described for woollen yarn in *par. 1 (d) above*. As camel hair has little felting quality, preparatory steeping is not necessary.

4. OTHER ANIMAL HAIRS, FURS AND WOOLS should be treated in one of the above three ways, according to the character of the fibre. Any kind of wool should be steeped before soap washing, if there are any doubts about its liability to felt, and it should never be subjected to violent changes of temperature while wet; never, for example, take it from very cold water and plunge it into very hot suds.

Hair yarns do not need steeping and, as a rule, need much lighter scouring because they retain less grease. A very little soap in a last rinse is usually an improvement.

5. LINEN. Natural flax colours vary considerably. The best Belgian flax is creamy in colour, often said to result from retting in the water of the river Lys; Russian flax is a very dark grey, and between these extremes there are many different shades.

If the natural colour is to be used, the yarn needs only to be softened; if it is to be made light or white, it must be bleached also.

(a) *Cleaning and softening*. Boil the yarn in a solution of good soap or soap flakes for an hour or so, cool it and rub the yarn vigorously; rinse and repeat the process until the yarn is soft.

(b) *Grass bleaching*. Lay the skeins out on grass in fine weather. Keep them damp and turn them occasionally. This takes weeks; it is said to be more permanent, and is the traditional method. It is not to be recommended in the soot-laden atmosphere of big cities.

(c) *Soap and Soda bleaching*. This is useful for obtaining a deep cream, light fawn or silvery grey – dependent on the original colour of the flax. The bleaching is done in a solution of 1 oz. soap and 1 oz. washing soda to 1 gallon of water (greater or smaller quantities in proportion). Soak the flax in three parts of the water and dissolve the soap and soda in the remaining part. Lift out the yarn, pour in the solution, stir well with a wooden or glass rod and return the flax. Bring it slowly to the boil and continue boiling for two hours, then let it cool in the liquid. If it is not light enough, mix a fresh solution to the same proportions and repeat the process until the desired shade is reached. Not more than four baths should be used, allowing the yarn to lie in the liquid for a day between each treatment.

(d) *Lime bleaching*. Provided it is carefully done, this very common method of bleaching is said to be perfectly safe. Make a stock solution by mixing chloride of lime with soft or rain water in the proportion of 2 oz. lime to 1 quart water. Put this in a tall bottle and allow it to settle for some hours.

Wash and soften the skeins (*par. 5 (a) above*), make a bleaching bath in the proportion of 1 part stock solution to 16 parts water ($\frac{1}{2}$ pint to the gallon) and lay in the wet skeins for two or three hours, moving them occasionally with a glass or wooden rod. The bath itself should be either earthenware, glass, or galvanized ware. Remove the yarn, expose it to the air for a few hours. Repeat the process until the yarn is sufficiently white. Never try to hurry this process by using a stronger solution – the yarn may be stained and tender places may develop later.

When the required shade is reached, rinse the skeins thoroughly and hang them to dry without artificial heat – out of doors for preference. The author has no personal experience of this method.

(e) *Using a proprietory bleaching solution*. There are many of these on the market nowadays, such as Parazone, Rayzone, etc. They all have some form of chlorinated lime as a basis, usually with alum or some similar substance to assist in precipitating the lime. They can be used with perfect safety in the proportion given in the directions for use in the same way as described for chloride of lime in *par. 5 (d) above*.

6. SILK. The only preparation needed for silk yarn is a light washing in olive oil soap (or Lux). Rinse the skeins and if it is a smooth spun yarn the skein should be *scrooped* to increase the lustre. Hang a skein on a smooth, strong rod which someone should hold. Put an equally smooth rod in the other end of the skein and twist it very tightly to wring out as

much moisture as possible (*Diagram* 79). Hang the skein to dry as described in *par. 1* (*d*) *above* for drying worsted yarn (*Diagram 78*). Rough-spun silk should not be scrooped and should be hung to dry as described for woollen yarn.

7. COTTON. Spun from cotton on the boll or on the seeds, the yarn needs only a light washing, unless it is desired to bleach it white. Cotton spun from machine carded slivers is, even at its best, darkened in colour a little by the imperfect removal of seed husk and other parts of the plant and, in some cases, it is quite a deep fawn.

(a) *Washing yarn spun from cotton slivers*. Soak the yarn in clean, soft water for about two hours. It should then be boiled for one hour in a solution of soap and soda; any good washing powder with a soap basis is suitable. Finally boil it in clear, soft water, rinse, squeeze or lightly mangle and hang the skeins to dry.

(b) *Bleaching*. One steeping in a bleaching solution made up as for linen (*pars. 5* (*d*) and (*e*) *above*) is usually sufficient to give an off-white shade to cotton spun from slivers and to make cotton spun from the seed a good white.

8. MIXTURE YARNS. Yarns containing wool must never be boiled in soap or soda. To bleach a mixture yarn of cotton and wool, use peroxide of hydrogen which will not harm the wool. The processes of scouring wool will do no harm to any of the natural fibres – silk, cotton, linen, hair, fur, etc.

Some spinners like to scour their fleece before using it for mixture yarns with silk or angora. It is still necessary to use olive oil when teasing or before combing, but it is, of course, easier to wash this out of the finished yarn than to scour out the natural grease.

9. SCOURING FLEECE. First tease the fleece well, then steep it and scour it exactly as described for wool yarns. The easiest way to handle the fleece is to tie it very loosely in thin muslin, knotted together at the top (*Diagram 80*). In each bath, untie the knots and move the fleece about a little, re-tying them to lift it into the next bath. When it is rinsed, spread it out to dry, preferably out of doors, if necessary with a net over it to prevent it from blowing about.

## Chapter Twelve

# MACHINE-SPUN YARNS

It would not be possible in a book of this kind to enter into details of the comparisons of hand and machine methods of spinning. All that can be attempted is to give the reader some indication of qualities and defects he may expect to find in yarns and to explain some of the reasons for them.

The processes of modern spinning are natural developments of the hand methods but, at all stages, they are more rigorous and less selective and there is always a tendency to prepare the material to suit the machine, instead of adapting the method to suit the material as does the hand craftsman.

Present-day spinning practices seem to be developing in the direction of finding one method suitable for all fibres, and to-day, wool, silk, cut synthetic fibres and even linen, can be spun on machinery directly developed from apparatus primarily designed for cotton. The reason for this undoubtedly lies in the ever-increasing production of mixture yarns from blended fibres. There are, of course, sound arguments in favour of well-blended yarns, but the melancholy fact remains that the most usual reasons for the practice are economic.

Before discussing mixture or any other yarns, it will be useful to know in what terms yarn size and construction is described.

1. YARN SIZES OR COUNTS. It is not enough to describe a yarn as 'thick' or 'thin' – the knitter wants to know how thick; the weaver must know how many yards he may expect to find in a given quantity. Having now become a spinner, you will readily understand how quickly one would be involved in astronomical figures if one had to describe every yarn as having so many yards in a pound; some of your own handspun yarns may well have 200 yards in 1 oz. Yet, in the course of centuries, a system of counting has grown up which tells both yardage

and number of yarns used to make the particular yarn being described.

A unit of length has been agreed on for each fibre – in the case of wool, for each type of spinning also – which is a hank or skein containing a certain number of yards; the number of such skeins required to weigh 1 lb. is the COUNT of the yarn.

For wool spun by the worsted method the unit is a skein of 560 yards; this means that if you have to spin 4 skeins of this length to make 1 lb., the size or count of your yarn is a 4s. The finer your yarn, the lighter in weight the skeins will be; to make up 1 lb., you may have to spin not 4, but 6 skeins and the size of this yarn will be 6s, i.e. the higher the count, the finer the yarn.

Now let us assume that this 6s single yarn is to be made into a 2-ply yarn. To do this, you will use the 6 skeins in pairs and you will finish the work with 3 skeins of 2-ply yarn which still weigh 1 lb. (roughly half the original yardage). The ply number is indicated in the count, usually – but unfortunately not invariably – in front of the size number of the singles, so your yarn will now be described as a 2/6s (or occasionally as 6s/2).

The various yarn counts are paragraphed below:

(a) *Worsted*. Number of skeins containing 560 yards required for 1 lb., for examples see above.

(b) *Woollen yarns:*

*Tweed*. Number of cuts containing 200 yards required for 1 lb. 9 cut = 9 × 200 yards per lb. Tweed yarns are always singles.

*Knitting and hosiery yarns*. (Yorkshire Count.) Number of hanks containing 256 yards required for 1 lb. (*see note at the end of this paragraph on 'Knitting yarns'*).

(c) *Cotton*. Number of hanks containing 840 yards required for 1 lb. The ply number follows the size number, viz. 8s/2 = 8 × 840 yards has been made into a 2-ply yarn; yardage per lb. = 8 × 840 ÷ 2.

(d) *Spun silk and spun synthetic fibres*. The unit is the same as for cotton, 840 yards; the size number indicates the number of skeins of the yarn per lb., irrespective of the ply number, which is sometimes placed before and sometimes after: viz. 2/25 (or 25/2) indicates that there are 25 skeins of 840 yards in 1 lb. and that it is a 2-ply yarn.

(e) *Thrown silk and continuous filament synthetic yarns.* The unit is the DENIER which is the weight in grammes of 9,000 metres or the weight in drams of 1,000 yards.

(f) *Linen.* Number of leas containing 300 yards required for 1 lb.

(g) *Fancy yarns.* These are usually cotton or rayon and the cotton count is used irrespective of whether they are plied or not. Thus, 8s Snarl = 8 × 840 yards per lb.

*Knitting yarns.* The handknitter is less interested in yardage per lb. than in size (in the sense of diameter), and these yarns are marketed not under count number but by the number of the ply; 2-ply, 3-ply, etc. The handspinner knows that good wool for woollen spinning is lofty (i.e. full), and therefore the better the wool the lighter in weight will be the yarn spun from it. In consequence a good quality 3-ply knitting wool will have a greater yardage per lb. than a lower quality, although the diameter of the yarn may be about the same.

In recent years, a curious misnomer has come into use to describe an exceedingly fine 2-ply yarn of a type first introduced from the Continent just before the last war. No doubt with the intention of emphasizing its fineness it is now described as 1-ply!

2. WOOL YARNS. What are wool yarns made from? Some of the answers to this may well surprise the reader even more than may the question.

Fleeces are only one of many forms in which wool reaches the yarn manufacturer; there is also the wool from the skins of sheep slaughtered for meat. This, known as fell wool, may be pulled from the skins or it may be removed with the aid of chemicals which do the work more quickly but are more harmful to the wool. For reasons which will presently be obvious, all the above are known as 'virgin' wool.

Next in importance as a source of supply is wool which is reclaimed in various ways. This reaches the spinners via the dustbin, the rag merchant, from waste cuttings in the clothing trades, loom waste and so on. It is sterilized, sorted and the best qualities – knitted goods, woven materials which have not been milled (i.e. felted up) – are torn up and eventually recarded and spun to make the class of yarn known as SHODDY.

Rags from lower quality wools, from milled materials, and from all the odds and ends that are unmixed with other fibres, are scratched to pieces by machines and the much-impoverished fibres are carded and spun into low quality yarns known as MUNGO.

But we have not yet touched bottom. There are still EXTRACT wool yarns. These are recovered from rags, in which wool is mixed with other fibres, by scratching them to pieces as for mungo, then treating them with sulphuric acid to destroy the other fibres. The wool fibres remain, by no means undamaged, but still sufficiently whole to allow them to be dignified by the name of wool.

Wool is made to suffer its final degradation in a class of yarns on which the trade has conferred the mellifluous name of ANGOLA. These are mixed yarns made from hard wool rags, any well-milled woollen rubbish, half rotten rags from rag-pickers. This conglomeration is torn, battered, cut and eventually scratched into a mass of fluff which is spun with cotton to make a soft yarn having what can only be described as whiskers.

It is not generally realized that practically all power-spun wool yarns contain some reclaimed wool, from the first quality yarns in which the proportion is low, to the yarns which have only enough virgin wool to make it possible to spin them at all.

The best qualities of virgin wools are used for higher grades of worsted and woollen yarns. Good Down wools go to the knitting and hosiery yarn spinners, the best of the Mountain wool is used for tweed yarns, and the coarser types of these and the Longwools are used in the carpet trade.

Apart from length of staple, the essential difference between wool chosen for worsted spinning and that used for woollen yarns is that these latter have better milling qualities, milling being the process of hot soap washing and felting woollen cloth to entangle the fibres of wool so that the material becomes a united mass of wool as well as a collection of interwoven yarns. Worsted yarns are usually woven into fabrics in which the weave shows clearly and with a certain smooth lustre; if they were milled, these characteristics would be lost and they are finished without being subjected to the rapid movement which so quickly felts wool. Even so, wool is selected for worsted yarns from the more lustrous types of fleece, which partly by reason of the larger scales and bigger crimp, have considerably less felting tendency.

*Worsted yarns* should be smooth, lustrous, strong, but not harsh, even in thickness and regular in spin and plying; fibres should be long and individually strong. Yarns of high count should show no coarse fibres.

Nowadays, worsted spinning can be done from much shorter wools than was formerly possible; even so, very short noils cannot be used in the making of worsted yarns and so they are carded with wool and spun into woollen yarns. Some so-called tweed yarns consist of this type of wool. They may be recognized by their shiny short fibres and somewhat hard handle, even when the spinning oil is washed out. They do not make a well consolidated woollen cloth.

*Tweed yarns* should be very elastic, lively in handle with reasonably long fibres which are springy and show strong, though not very small crimp. Whether fibres are coarse or fairly fine will depend on the variety of tweed; Harris yarns from the West Highland type of Blackface are coarser than Cheviot yarns. Mungo yarns sometimes make their appearance as 'Cheviot type' tweed yarn, or simply as 'tweed yarn'. They are recognizable by the short, weak fibres with feeble crimp and the yarn lacks elasticity – though this may be disguised a little by tight spinning. Mungo, even extract wool, is sometimes used in nondescript tweed yarns, mixed with some virgin wool. The contrast between the two types of fibre is usually quite obvious when the yarn is picked apart for examination.

*Fine woollen yarns* should show fine stapled wool of reasonable length. The yarn should be full, round, even in thickness, regular in spin with no twits (thin and therefore over-spun places). Very short noils from worsted wools are sometimes spun into fine woollen yarns; they are usually hard and rather tightly twisted, but so long as one recognizes them for what they are, good use can be made of them. They will not felt well and if used for dress material it needs finishing, like any other worsted, by crabbing. Low grades of reclaimed wool are sometimes mixed with some virgin wool for fine woollen yarns. They are inelastic, with somewhat solid handle, often overspun and never worth using for handweaving.

*Carpet and rug yarns*, so described, are not always all wool or even wool at all. Good wool rug yarns should be long stapled wool, lustrous and full, and above all the fibres should be strong; whether coarse or fine fibred depends on the class of yarn – fine yarn, fine fibre is a good general rule. Wool yarn for pile rugs should certainly be finer than for tapestry rugs and length of fibres is less important than fullness of yarn since it is the cross section which will show and take the wear.

*Angora (rabbit) wool* yarns are almost always spun with some wool. Good yarns do not have long projections of coarse angora fibres; the character of these projections gives some indication of the quality of angora used. Short soft whiskers are characteristic of good yarns. The coarse hairs not only shed off the knitted or woven fabric, they have an unpleasant effect on the colour if the yarn is dyed to a dark shade because they accept dyestuff less readily than the wool and finer fibres.

N.B. *Never buy wool which is spotted with mildew; these spots develop into weak places within a very short time.*

3. COTTON YARNS. Cotton for machine spinning is picked and immediately put through a machine called a gin to remove the seeds and the lints – these are very short fibres which are now used in the manufacture of rayon yarns. The raw cotton, which still contains plant waste, dust and other foreign matter, is baled and in this form it reaches the manufacturers. Here it is opened out and cleaned in various machines and is then carded and made into slivers (a continuous length of slightly drawn fibres); for fine yarns the slivers are combed in a machine which removes short fibres and straightens out the long ones. The slivers are further drawn out through another series of machines to make the roving from which the yarn itself is spun.

If very smooth yarns are wanted, they are passed quickly through a flame which singes off projecting fibres. These are known as GASSED yarns.

Cotton (and linen) can be made lustrous by immersing it in a solution of caustic soda and stretching it tightly. This actually alters the structure of the fibres, the yarn is slightly lengthened, it becomes stronger, lustrous and develops a higher affinity for dyestuffs. This is the process known as MERCERIZATION.

The best yarns are spun from Sea Island and Egyptian cotton. Both are long and fine stapled. Egyptian cotton is a heavy cream colour, American cotton which is much shorter and coarser is a good deal whiter.

A good cotton yarn should be smooth, not fluffy, even in size and regular in spin and plying, free from 'neps' – hard bits of fluff – and clean. Many low grade cottons which have been imperfectly cleaned show dark flecks in the yarns. These do not bleach out, often they will not take dye, and material woven from them is marred by a slightly dirty appearance.

4. LINEN. A good linen yarn for warp should be evenly spun with long fibred flax. It should be supple, free from fluffiness, and above all free from unhackled lumps.

Weft linen is often spun from the shorter fibres, the better qualities of tow. In the high counts they are, naturally, less satisfactory than in the coarser yarns. It is almost impossible to use such yarn for warp, even when sized.

Fine singles yarns spun from line are in very short supply and a compromise is effected by spinning a 2-ply tow yarn which is marketed as a warp yarn.

5. SILK. (Allow no one to describe rayon as 'silk' in your presence!) The qualities to be desired in nett silk are all such as one would expect. Perfection of lustre, absolutely regularity, freedom from even the slightest roughness, including the minute knots used to mend single filaments.

Spun silk yarns should show reasonable fibre length, lustre, and – unless designed as 'rough-spun' – absolute regularity of spin in both singles and plying. They should be free from fluffs and other roughnesses. Undyed yarns vary in colour considerably; some are almost corn coloured. This is dependent on the breed of silkworm used and is not an indication of quality, either good or bad.

6. MIXTURE YARNS. Here one can give little guidance. As stated above, almost all yarns are mixtures to-day and if, for purposes of dyeing or for some other reason, it is necessary to discover the content of a yarn, one has no alternative to applying careful chemical tests. A description

of such tests is quite outside the scope of this book, but the following notes on simple, somewhat rough-and-ready methods may prove to be of some use.

## 7. IDENTIFYING YARNS BY SIMPLE TESTS.

*Caustic Soda.* A solution gives one some useful information. Cotton, linen, hemp, jute turn to yellow or brown when boiled in it; rayons swell; silk and all animal fibres dissolve.

*Burning tests.* Wool, silk and all other animal fibres burn with a smell of a blacksmith's shop or burnt feathers. They are consumed very slowly and a tiny bead is left at the end of the fibre.

All vegetable fibres flame up quickly with a smell of burnt paper. They leave a white ash.

Viscose rayon burns, like cotton, very quickly; acetate rayon burns less quickly and melts into little balls which stay on the end of the yarn. Nylon burns rather slowly and melts very quickly.

# SOME USEFUL BOOKS

## ON HANDSPINNING

*Methods of Handspinning in Egypt and the Sudan.* G. Crowfoot. 1931. (Bankfield Museum, Halifax.)

*Hand Wool Combing.* H. Ling Roth. (Bankfield Museum, Halifax.)

*A Complete Guide to Handspinning.* K. Grassett. (London School of Weaving.)

*Navajo Shepherd and Weaver.* G. Reichard. (Augustin, New York.)


## ON SHEEP

*The Handbook of the National Sheepbreeders' Association.* 1952.

*Sheep.* J. F. Thomas. 1945. (Faber.)

*Sheep Farming.* Sir Alan Fraser. 1945. (Lockwood.)

*Sheep Husbandry.* Sir Alan Fraser. 1950. (Lockwood.)


## MISCELLANEOUS

*Wool Sorting.* Mark and Peter Prior. (Dryad Press.)

*The Linen Trade of Europe in the Spinning Wheel Period.* John Horner of Belfast. 1920. (Contains many excellent drawings of spinning wheels.)

*Silk.* Luther Hooper. (Pitman.)

*So Spins the Silkworm.* Zoe, Lady Hart Dyke (of Lullingstone Silk Farm, Kent.) (Rockliff.)

*Angora Wool Production.* J. MacDougall (Watmoughs.)


## ON YARN MANUFACTURE, ETC.

*Introduction to the Study of Spinning.* W. E. Morton. 1952. Ed. (Longmans, Green & Co.)

*A History of Wool and Wool Combing.* Joseph Burnley.

*Woollen and Worsted Raw Materials.* J. R. Hind. 1948. Ed. (Benn.)

*The World of Cotton.* E. Vale. 1952. (Robert Hale.)

*Standard Handbook of Textiles.* A. J. Hall. (United Trade Press.)

*Textile Fibres and Their Uses.* K. Hess. (Lippincott, New York.)

*Textiles On Test.* J. C. Williams. (Chapman & Hall.)

# INDEX